W9-BTI-717

# ORGANIZATIONAL COMMUNICATION

## AN INTRODUCTION TO COMMUNICATION AND HUMAN RELATION STRATEGIES

KEN W. WHITE
ELWOOD N. CHAPMAN

PEARSON CUSTOM PUBLISHING

EMERSON COLLEGE LIBRARY

HM
131
.W458
1999

Cover Art: Dave Cutler / Spots on the Spot!
Cover Design: Caldera Design, Phoenix, AZ

Excerpts from:

*Your Attitude Is Showing*, Eighth Edition,
by Elwood N. Chapman
Copyright © 1996 by Prentice-Hall, Inc.
A Pearson Education Company
Upper Saddle River, New Jersey 07458

This special edition published in cooperation with
Pearson Custom Publishing

Copyright © 1997 by Simon & Schuster Custom Publishing
Copyright © 1999 by Pearson Custom Publishing
All rights reserved.

Permission in writing must be obtained from the publisher before any
part of this work may be reproduced or transmitted in any form or by
any means, electronic or mechanical, including photocopying and
recording, or by any information storage or retrieval system.

Printed in the United States of America

18 17 16 15 14 13 12 11 10 9

*Please visit our website at www.pearsoncustom.com*

ISBN 0–536–00203–7
BA 990124

PEARSON CUSTOM PUBLISHING
160 Gould Street/Needham Heights, MA 02194
A Pearson Education Company

# ◆ CONTENTS

# ◆ AN OPEN LETTER TO UNIVERSITY OF PHOENIX STUDENTS

This is the second edition of *Organizational Communication: An Introduction to Communication and Human Relation Strategies*. It was prepared especially for students enrolled in **MGT 331: Organizational Behavior** through the collaborative effort of a University of Phoenix faculty member, who specializes in communication, and a renowned author of one of the most highly regarded primers in the field of business human relations.

The book reflects the University of Phoenix's purpose to assist working adults in the achievement of their personal, professional, and career goals in a manner consistent with integrating academic theory and practical application. It recognizes the principles of adult learning through its underlying philosophy of applied problem-solving in the educational process.

The book facilitates learning by combining the skills of a faculty member with advanced academic preparation and an author with current professional experience. It is intended as a supplementary text and as a practical handbook for future reference.

Like the University of Phoenix, we hope that *Organizational Communication* provides a rich learning experience that is essential in the development of your ability to communicate effectively, to reason both abstractly and concretely, and to understand and engage in the process of critical thinking.

We join with the University in helping you to achieve these important educational objectives!

We invite your comments on this book, regarding both its strengths and areas that may need improvement. We would like to hear from you so that we can continue writing about concepts and techniques you find valuable, and so that we can add information to areas in the book that you feel are presently underdeveloped or missing. Please send any ideas, or simply your greetings, to us care of Undergraduate Business and Management Programs, University of Phoenix, 4615 East Elwood Street, Phoenix, Arizona 85040, or email us at kenwhite@ctc.edu or white_kenw@msn.com.

Good luck!

*Ken White*
*Elwood Chapman*

# ◆ PREFACE

This book contains ideas that have been used in the classroom and workplace for almost thirty years to train both new and experienced employees. The information contained in these pages has helped individuals of all ages and backgrounds play their communication and human relations roles with greater understanding and sensitivity.

As a recent collaboration between the two authors, *Organizational Communication* also offers a new way of looking at communication in organizations. Instead of focusing on the typical approach that sees communication simply as the transmission of information, the communication theory and practical ideas presented in this book are *relational*. Organizational communication is treated as an inherently human relations process, one that is not reducible to "sending and receiving" or "codes and messages." We emphasize how organizational members co-create (or co-damage) working relationships as they communicate. It assumes that effective communication and positive working relationships are inseparable. They go hand-in-hand!

This book is intended as an introduction for working adults who want practical ideas and skills that will help them communicate more effectively with their co-workers. It is not meant for advanced theoretical study. But unlike so-called self-help books, it does not ignore conceptual issues or reduce communication and human relation effectiveness to techniques or formulas. Of course, we offer practical tips on how to improve your communication and human relations skills, but we also recognize that there is much more to good communication and human relations than simply following our tips. We assume that our readers are thoughtful individuals who are committed to improving their lives and are capable of judging how the concepts and suggestions in this book apply to their own situations.

Effective communication and human relations require lifelong learning. They are the skills by which you make your way through school, work, and life. Your ability to effectively communicate and relate with people largely determines the quality of your whole life and your personal happiness.

---

*Effective communication and human relations make life work!*

---

As you read and study *Organizational Communication,* keep in mind that people who balance their communication skills with human relations competencies find greater on-the-job happiness, contribute more to the productivity of organizations, and in general have more successful careers.

These points are supported throughout the book. The purpose of the chapters in Part One is to offer some basic ideas that help readers apply a communication perspective to the rest of the book. The first chapter introduces readers to the complexity of communication. Chapter 2 emphasizes the role of relational communication in organizations and sets the stage for a discussion of choice in communication behaviors in Chapter 3. Chapter 4 concludes Part One with a way to develop effective communication choices.

The goal of the chapters in Part Two is to provide readers with information on the role of social organization in communication and working relations. Chapters 5 through 7 concentrate on the nature and structure of working relationships. Chapter 8 focuses on communication and success as a team player.

Chapters in Part Three suggest that communication is a means for coping with such organizational challenges as stress, poor working relationships, testing, and conflict.

Part Four addresses the area of organizational change and communication. It implies that effective communication helps employees deal with new job situations, diversified workplaces, computer-based communication, and the difficult issue of constructive feedback.

The book concludes with Part Five, which discusses communication and career development issues. For example, Chapter 17 suggests how to avoid a number of common communication and human relations mistakes that can damage career opportunities. Chapters 18 through 20 deal with issues of competence and career planning.

A book like this is never written by the authors alone. Ken would like to acknowledge the people who have contributed in direct and indirect ways to his part of this book. His most important living relationships—with his wife, Liz, sons Nathan and Jamie, and other immediate family members—are the central reasons for his need to continually learn and write this book. He especially appreciates Liz reading numerous drafts and helping to clarify his thoughts and words. In that regard, his friend and colleague, Chad Lewis, supported him with his ideas and enthusiasm throughout the writing process.

He thanks former professors John Stewart, Jody Nyquist, and Teri Albrecht for inspiring his interest in this subject, and for introducing him to many of the ideas in this book. (John's advice to learn to "live within the tension" remains poignant.)

Thanks also to many colleagues at the University of Phoenix, especially Beth Aguiar and Nancy Blankinship, for encouraging this project. Jon Baillie of Simon and Schuster has also been extremely cooperative. Finally, thanks to all past and future students (and readers) who have challenged his ideas and continue to prompt him to grow.

# ◆PART ONE

---

## UNDERSTANDING
## ORGANIZATIONAL COMMUNICATION

---

Most of our communication takes place in organizations. You are preparing right now to communicate with other students in the organizational setting of a college course. We communicate every day in such diverse organizations as our families, educational institutions, corporations, industrial businesses, social service agencies, governmental departments, church meetings, and special interest groups. Some organizational theorists maintain that *all* communication is done in organizational settings!

---

*You have a need to communicate more effectively*
*in organizations in all areas of your life.*

---

The purpose of this section of the book is to introduce you to the theory of *organizational communication*. Although the book is intended to be practical, we believe that "good theory is good practice." But if you cannot translate theory into practical ideas, it may not be a good theory. We will attempt to make sure that there is a direct relationship between theory and practice in each chapter of this book. We have also limited theoretical information to the kind and amount we feel is appropriate for undergraduate students. But it is difficult and cumbersome to point out the direct relationship between theory and practice in each individual case. Therefore, Chapter 4 of this section of the book will suggest a way for you to begin judging the usefulness of communication and human relations information yourself.

There are a number of theories of organizational communication. For the purposes of this book, we offer an overview of three—*bureaucratic theory, human relations theory,* and *systems theory.*

## ◆ THE BUREAUCRATIC THEORY OF ORGANIZATIONAL COMMUNICATION

Every organizational theory has something to say about communication. Bureaucratic theory is about *control* based on rational rules that regulate the entire organization. Written documents—organizational charts, corporate manuals, operating instructions, job descriptions, and such—establish guidelines for virtually all organizational activities. There is a clear, firm, orderly system of hierarchy. Fields of responsibilities are clearly delineated for employees in the organization. There is little room for flexibility.

---

*In this book, we identify the bureaucratic theory of organizational*
*communication with what we call "command" communication.*

---

Bureaucratic communication is mostly downward. Lower levels typically respond with reports. For example, field representatives meet with their sales managers to receive information about what users tell them concerning problems with the organization's products.

There is typically almost no concern for horizontal communication in the bureaucratic theory. Regarding the above example, if sales people in different sections of the organization do exchange ideas, it is almost always through a higher level of management.

This theory is attributed to Max Weber's ideas. Weber is recognized as having developed the single most powerful theory of organization. Bureaucratic theory has been the starting point for almost all thinking in organizational theory.

## ◆ THE HUMAN RELATIONS THEORY OF ORGANIZATIONAL COMMUNICATION

Human relations theory is based on the concept that an organization not only has the function of producing a product or service, but also needs to fulfill the employees' needs for such things as job satisfaction. Human relations theory is about *people* who are more responsive to other members of their organization than they are to the controls and incentives of management. There are written documents to guide activities of the organization, but they do not cover the complexity or uncertainty of human relations. Because human relations is often less rational, there is a need for significantly more flexibility.

---

*In this book, we identify the human relations theory of organizational communication with what we call "relational" communication.*

---

Human relations theory emphasizes that organizational communication is largely oral, either impersonal or interpersonal. There is less emphasis on written directives, memos, or such. Communication is seen as less formal—managers talk with employees face-to-face or over e-mail to inform them of a new procedure. That is in contrast to formal communication where managers might present instructions at structured meetings to their employees.

Much of the communication in human relations theory is horizontal. For example, one employee in production will see a way to reduce the loud noise in a shop and talk it over with co-workers in similar shops. From these horizontal exchanges comes the need to call meetings about the problem, to present the idea to others who would be involved in the changes, and to gather additional suggestions.

Human relations theory sees horizontal communication as more casual discussions than the organized deliberations of downward communication.

The human relations theory of organizational communication was developed primarily at the Harvard School of Business. It was sparked by the realization that people form informal groups within an organization—groups that communicate outside of, and often in spite of, detailed organizational plans. These groups are quite powerful and very valuable to the organization. Although the point may seem obvious to us today, it was a significant realization in the 1940s.

Human relations is really the area of this book's expertise. Elwood is the author of one of the most highly regarded primers in the field of business human relations in the country. Ken has a Ph.D. in speech communication from the University of Washington in the area of interpersonal communication, and has taught organizational behavior and human relations from a communication perspective in colleges and universities like the University of Phoenix for a number of years. We have come together because communication skills are *the way* to put human relations ideas into organizational practice!

## ◆ THE SYSTEMS THEORY OF ORGANIZATIONAL COMMUNICATION

Systems theory is based on the view that an organization is a system of behaviors composed of subsystems that have definite limits within the system. Subsystems interact with other subsystems and individual behaviors are dependent on their relationships to various subsystems.

---

*In this book, we identify the systems theory of organizational communication with the dynamic between "command" and "relational" communication, the area where individual judgment or a "systems competency" is needed to understand the complexity and ambiguity of organizational interrelationships.*

---

Systems theory maintains that there is no "best way" to structure or to communicate within an organization. Instead, structure and communication vary depending on such *contingencies* as the personalities and needs of the people in the organization; the goals, responsibilities, duties, and tasks of the organization; the relationships of the employees; and the larger structure of the communication climate of the organization.

According to systems theory, communication generally flows downward in organizations, as when managers issue "commands." For example, the vice-president of marketing calls a meeting for all sales personnel in order to tell them of innovations for responding to potential customers who resist purchases.

But for some organizations, systems theory recognizes that contingencies determine that communication is upward—employees suggest to management procedures for reducing the cost of producing a product or service. Still other organizations depend largely on horizontal communication. For example, the manager of the inventory department communicates with the manager of the shipping department to gather ideas for a policy on holiday schedules.

In systems theory, information and procedures interact with people to affect communication. "Put it in writing" may be the instruction of one manager who is promoted; "give me your ideas face-to-face" may be the instruction of her replacement. Organizational communication is complex because people are often ambiguous and procedures often change.

##  THE PURPOSE OF PART ONE OF THIS BOOK

The purpose of the chapters in Part One of the book is *to help you see organizational communication differently and to begin thinking how you can develop the necessary communication attitudes and skills to make effective choices when dealing with information and people.*

Chapter 1 will discuss the complexity of organizational communication, introduce the "command" function of communication, and suggest ways to improve feedback and active listening. Chapter 2 will extend these ideas by moving beyond the area of organizational commands and stressing the importance of informal communication and human relations. While we think of command communication (bureaucratic) as being intentional, purposeful, and rational, "relational" communication illustrates that communication is inevitable and organizational members "cannot NOT communicate."

Chapter 3 emphasizes that better commands and relations are the result of effectively coping with the uncertainties and ambiguities of organizational communication. In turn, more effective coping is the result of better communication choices. Chapter 4 concludes Part One with a model of "communication competence" that is intended to help you begin to develop and take control of those choices.

As we move from the abstractions of theory to the practicalities of communicating, keep in mind that the first—the essential—guide to getting the most out of this book is this two-step secret of communication success:

1. *Be open to learning and new ideas.*

2. *See communication improvement as a "way of living."*

Being open to learning doesn't mean that you have to believe everything in this book. It simply means trying to become aware of how your own past ideas and experiences (what we call your "horizon of experiences") can interfere with your *openness* to different ideas. To be open is not to be gullible; it is to be thoughtful.

A "way of living" means that you extend the *thoughtfulness* necessary to be open to the ideas in this book to your whole life. The quality of your whole life, not just your organizational life, is determined by the quality of your communication. If you want to improve your organizational communication, you must also think about areas such as your family communication. The tips and techniques to be presented in this book are only as good as the attitudes, values, and beliefs that influence your whole life.

# ◆ CHAPTER 1

## WHAT IS THIS THING CALLED COMMUNICATION?

Effective communication is an essential part of success in the workplace.

Managers spend up to 80 percent of their day communicating.

Often it is a subordinate's communication skills that determine success or failure in critical situations.

Consequently, both employers and employees place high value on communication skills. Effective communication is a requirement for effective performance appraisal, coping with conflict and stress, motivation of subordinates, decision-making, leadership, and other important human relations skills. In fact, effective communication and human relations are the cornerstones of organizational effectiveness.

Unfortunately, confusion regarding effective communication is common in all types of organizations across all organizational levels. Often, managers and subordinates do not even agree on whether they have met during the week! Up to 95 percent of high-ranking managers report believing they have a good grasp of employee problems, yet only about 30 percent of subordinates agree that they do.

Confusion about effective communication is understandable in light of the complexity associated with what many people consider to be the simple transmission of messages. In this chapter, we will offer a *functional* definition of communication within an organizational context as offered by Charles Conrad, a noted organizational communication scholar. Conrad defines communication as the process through which people issue, receive, interpret, and act on *commands,* and through which people create and maintain productive business and personal *relationships* with other members of the organization. But before proceeding with the implications of this two-fold definition, we need to think about the complexity of communication and why a functional approach may be useful.

## ◆ THE COMPLEXITY OF COMMUNICATION

The word *communication* is defined differently by many different disciplines and possesses many different meanings. In fact, seeking a single working definition of communication may not be as productive as identifying the major components behind the idea. The concept *communication* is used legitimately in a number of ways. For example, the communication theorist Frank Dance has identified 15 distinct conceptual components in various definitions. Table 1.1 shows how Stephen Littlejohn summarizes the components and provides an example of each.

Obviously, it is a problem to provide a precise definition of communication. But a more productive question we can pursue for the purposes of this book concerns how we should distinguish communication from other forms of behavior in an organization. One way of looking at the above definitions and everything that happens when a person engages in communication is to identify two general functions of communication that relate directly to organizations. Again, Conrad has identified these functions as:

1. The command function

2. The relational function

This approach assumes that in some ways communication *functions* as a tool for members of organizations to issue, receive, interpret, and act on commands, and to create and maintain productive business and personal relationships. (By "command," we mean any message that influences other people to take action or to accept certain ideas. As we will suggest, a command is not necessarily an order. It can also be a statement, question, or request.)

In the following section, we will discuss the command function of communication and its reliance on feedback and active listening. The chapter will conclude with some comments on the limitations of this type of communication. In Chapter 2, we will deal with the relational nature of communication.

## ◆ THE COMMAND FUNCTION OF COMMUNICATION

The command perspective on communication assumes that people communicate effectively only when they choose both to initiate action and to limit their actions in clearly prescribed ways.

The communication process begins when one person wants to *transmit information* to another person.

That's why this approach can be likened to the popular *sender-receiver model of communication.* From this perspective, a member of an organization issues messages or "commands," which tell other members to take action and to limit that action to a particular series of steps to be taken at a specified time and at a specified place. This desire to transmit this kind of information is usually conscious, rational, and eventually expressed using oral or written language—in other words, instructions and publications.

**TABLE 1.1 CONCEPTUAL COMPONENTS IN COMMUNICATION**

| | | |
|---|---|---|
| 1. | Symbols/Verbal/Speech: | "Communication is the verbal interchange of thought or idea." |
| 2. | Understanding: | "Communication is the process by which we understand others and in turn endeavor to be understood by them. It is dynamic, constantly changing and shifting in response to the total situation." |
| 3. | Interaction Relationship/ Social Process: | "Interaction, even on the biological level, is a kind of communication; otherwise common acts could not occur." |
| 4. | Reduction of Uncertainty: | "Communication arises out of the need to reduce uncertainty, to act effectively, to defend or strengthen the ego." |
| 5. | Process: | "Communication: the transmission of information, idea, emotion, skills, etc., by the use of symbols—words, pictures, figures, graphs, etc. It is the act or process of transmission that is usually called communication." |
| 6. | Transfer Transmission/ Interchange: | "The connecting thread appears to be the idea of something being transferred from one thing, or person, to another. We use the word 'communication' sometimes to refer to what is so transferred, sometimes to the means by which it is transferred, sometimes to the whole process. In many cases, what is transferred in this way continues to be shared; if I convey information to another person, it does not leave my own possession through coming into his. Accordingly, the word 'communication' acquires also the sense of participation. It is in this sense, for example, that religious worshipers are said to communicate." |
| 7. | Linking/Binding: | "Communication is the process that links discontinuous parts of the living world to one another." |
| 8. | Commonality: | "It (communication) is a process that makes common to two or several what was the monopoly of one or some." |

| | | |
|---|---|---|
| 9. | Channel/Carrier/Means/ Route: | "The means of sending military messages, orders, etc., as by telephone, telegraph, radio, couriers." |
| 10. | Replicating Memories: | "Communication is the process of conducting the attention of another person for the purpose of replicating memories." |
| 11. | Discriminative Behavior/ Modifying Response: | "Communication is the discriminatory response of an organism to a stimulus." |
| 12. | Stimuli: | "Every communication act is viewed as a transmission of information, consisting of a discriminative stimuli, from a source to a recipient." |
| 13. | Intentional: | "In the main, communication has as its central interest those behavioral situations in which a source transmits a message to a receiver *with conscious intent to affect the latter's behaviors.*" |
| 14. | Time /Situation: | "The communication process is one of transition from one structured situation-as-a-whole to another, in preferred design." |
| 15. | Power: | "Communication is the mechanism by which power is exerted." |

For example, instructions are oral commands, generally given in a face-to-face encounter and addressed to a single person or clearly identified group of persons. Instructions are highly flexible commands that seem to be transient rather than permanent. They are viewed as being linked to a specific problem, which is relatively new, rare, or unprecedented, and are from an individual rather than from the organization.

In contrast, publications create the impression that the command is directed to a general audience. If no one has been picked out as the recipient, the message seems addressed to anyone and everyone. Publications also create the impression that the command is official; that is, it is written by the organization or by someone who represents the organization rather than by any one individual. Finally, publications suggest both that the command is a relatively permanent injunction and, indirectly, that the problem it addresses is important and recurring.

Regardless of the communication vehicle used, the command function begins with a perception—a thought or a feeling—which must be encoded before it can be transmitted. "Encoding" literally means to put a message "into code." A

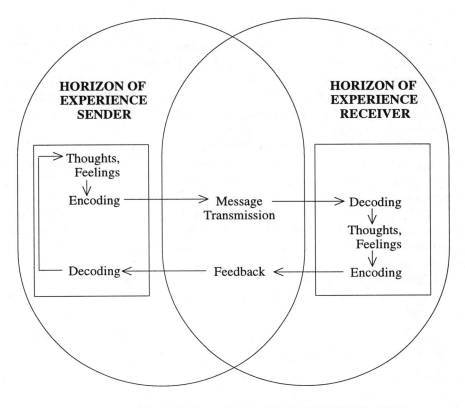

**FIGURE 1.1 SENDER-RECEIVER MODEL OF COMMUNICATION**

sender puts a message into code using oral, nonverbal, and written means. After transmission, the receiver must decode the message. After decoding, the message is then transformed into a perception—another thought or a feeling—on the part of the receiver.

What is most important for the communication of a command to function properly is that the entire process is repeated when the receiver provides *feedback*. Feedback occurs during this two-way communication when a receiver responds to the original sender of a message.

We will talk more about feedback in a moment. But in reviewing the command function it should be quite apparent that even very simple messages can be hampered because many parts of the communication process are private and not shared (e.g., thoughts and feelings, encoding, decoding). Only the actual oral or written transmission of a message is received—the *horizon of experience* of communicators influences the achievement of meaning. "Horizon of experience" is broadly defined here to include perceptions, values, prejudices, biases, culture, attitudes, and opinions derived from language and previous experience. Consequently, the command function of communication relies on processes of persuasion and influence. Its effectiveness depends on the availability of some form of influence, and communication strategies through which members of organizations persuade other members to act in specific ways.

Different understandings occur partly because of the difficulty of understanding another person's culture, language, personal experiences, or feelings. For example, if you think that another person is angry with you, you may perceive an angry message, even if the person is not really angry. You may find yourself needing to communicate differently—in other words, persuasively. Persuasion, at one level, is the desire to influence others. Effective persuasion depends on our ability to sense the situation that we are in and to adjust our communication accordingly.

Communication in a court of law differs from communication on a basketball court because people know from experience that these "courts" are very different. You have to communicate differently in a quiet restaurant than in a noisy bus station.

To summarize, the command function of communication (or the sender-receiver model) is useful in that it presents communication as a multidimensional process involving conscious and logical steps:

- *Encoding*—Puts a thought or idea into a code that is understandable to another person and can be transmitted.

- *Transmitting*—The act of sending out the signal or message. This is a physical action normally done with vocal cords, mouth, or nonverbal action.

- *Receiving*—The action where a sensory organ of the body collects the signals or messages.

- *Decoding*—This action takes the signal or message and makes some sense of it.

- *Feedback*—This essential element confirms to the sender of the message that it has been received and was or was not clearly understood.

- *Horizon of Experience*—Includes perceptions, values, prejudices, biases, culture, attitudes, and opinions derived from language and previous experience. It is what affects our understandings.

In addition, the model helps us to appreciate the complexity associated with the sending and receiving of even simple messages.

On the other hand, the rationality of the command or sender-receiver model does not capture the full richness of communication, nor does it account for all the dynamics of communication. The ideas offered in the previous paragraphs just begin to "scratch the surface." But while simply understanding the complexity of the communication process does not, by itself, improve communication, the command perspective does offer some suggestions for improving the clarity of messages. Let's take a look at a couple of these techniques before we discuss the limitations of the command function.

**Feedback and Active Listening**

As mentioned earlier, in order for the command function to be effective, it must involve the production of adequate feedback about the actions that actually are taken by people who have been issued commands.

Supervisors often *assume* that their subordinates will carry out their commands.

This assumption is especially strong when the supervisor has issued a set of routine instructions. Comfortable in the knowledge that their commands will be carried out, supervisors instruct other people to take actions which, when completed, will allow the task that the particular work unit has taken on to be accomplished. If any of the people who are involved in the command process fail to carry out the commands they were given properly or promptly, the supervisor will need to modify the commands that were given to the other people involved.

---

*Supervisors cannot make these adjustments unless they receive prompt and accurate feedback about the extent to which each of their commands has been carried out.*

---

Feedback involves the timely and appropriate practice of active listening, which improves the achievement of understanding between communicators.

Imagine a situation involving one-way communication where you can only receive information without being allowed to provide feedback. You would be unable to ask questions to clarify a communicator's intent. You would not be able to add to the other person's understanding of the topic being discussed. The situation described would be much like being prohibited from asking questions of a speaker—you might not understand the material being covered and the speaker might be completely unaware of your lack of understanding.

The command function of communication depends on *two-way communication*, which provides for feedback, which improves understanding. This is true, because with feedback there is an opportunity to correct, or to otherwise refine, communication leading to mutual understanding and agreement. Clearly, feedback should be encouraged whenever communication functions to transmit commands.

---

*A lack of feedback significantly affects the quality of oral instructions and written publications.*

---

Problems with the communication process interfere with interpretation of directives and orders. Consequently, managers improve the effectiveness of their commands by encouraging two-way communication.

Generally, managers should actively solicit and provide feedback from subordinates, customers, or anyone else affected by or who influences their position. While we will discuss the principles of constructive feedback in a later chapter, we would like to make a few more general suggestions at this point. Two communication techniques that improve two-way communication are paraphrasing and perception checking. Paraphrasing and perception checking are active listening skills. This is an appropriate term, because active listening skills supplement and enhance basic listening for the purpose of clarifying meaning and providing better feedback.

Paraphrasing and perception checking involve communication that helps the sender to clarify literal communication or intent and improves the quality of feedback.

1. *Practice paraphrasing.* "Paraphrasing" is a concise response to a speaker that states the essence of the other's content in the listener's own words. It involves repeating back in your own words what you thought you heard the sender or speaker say.

   Different working interpretations in communication sometimes make it hard to understand a message, particularly a long and/or complex communication.

   The objective of paraphrasing is to insure that the receiver got the sense of the message the sender actually sent. Consequently, a good paraphrase is concise. When people start to use this skill, they are often too wordy. If it is as long or longer than the speaker's own words, the message can be lost.

   In addition, a good paraphrase summarizes the speaker's message. It cuts through the clutter and focuses on the essence of the speaker's ideas. This will require that you develop a sense of what is central to a speaker's message. One way of doing this is by focusing on the content of the speaker's message. As we will discuss further in Chapter 2, emotion is a legitimate part of communication, but when one is trying to paraphrase it is more productive to deal with the facts rather than the emotions of the message.

   By focusing on the speaker's message and repeating the speaker's words back in your own words, you show an understanding of the speaker's frame of reference or horizon of experience. Remember, paraphrasing is different than "parroting" (repeating exactly the speaker's words).

   Most of us know from experience that communication is unreliable unless checked out. Paraphrasing greatly reduces the likelihood of poor listening and unresponsive feedback.

2. *Check Perception.* "Perception checking" is similar to paraphrasing, but one difference is that perception checking is about feelings more than facts. Here, the focus is upon checking out what you perceive to be the emotions that motivate another person's communication. Here, the concern isn't with

what the person communicated (words) as much as it is with what the other person conveys (tone) and means.

Listeners frequently miss many of the emotional dimensions of a conversation. Consequently, they miss the speaker's personal reaction to the events being described. As philosopher William James put it, "Individuality is found in feeling." If we miss the feelings, we miss the opportunity to sense the unique situation of the speaker. Feelings also help us sort our data, organize it, and use it effectively as we shape and share relevant feedback.

For example, an employee might be consistently late to work. You might assume from this "communication" that the employee doesn't care much about his or her job. If you checked out this perception, you might find that the employee was previously punctual and cares a great deal about his or her job, but is extremely frustrated. The feeling of frustration could lead you to the understanding that the problem is a temporary one associated with the city transit system.

## The Limitations of the Sender-Receiver Model

Although we recognize that sending a person a letter, memo, report, and even a face-to-face instruction consists of encoding and decoding messages, it would be a mistake to see that as the only function of communication.

Sending messages is never as simple as the transfer of meaning from one person to another.

The point is crucial because the process of communication involves so much more than simple mechanics and that makes it virtually impossible to achieve trouble-free communication.

---

*Communication "problems" are normal because communication always involves other people and people are always different.*

---

Consequently, when confronting typical communication challenges in organizations, such as a command not being interpreted the "correct" way, it easily becomes frustrating to pursue questions like "What's the right way?" It may be more productive to ask questions like "What are my other choices?" In other words, it is important to understand that effective communication is not simply a matter of good mechanics—the correct way—but a matter of dealing with people themselves.

For example, meanings are in people, not in words. Words do not have meanings, people do. Sure, you can go to the dictionary and look up a word's meaning, but the dictionary never supplies a context for using the word. We do not get meanings from words; we give meanings to words. We attribute meanings based upon our own frame of reference or "horizon of experience," not on the other person's frame of reference. Consequently, communication is a two-way process where simply saying something correctly to another person is not the whole story. Communication is understanding ourselves, other people, and the situations in which we find each other.

---

*Effective communication is also a consequence of the choices we make about people and situations. It's about human relations.*

---

Many of our day-to-day communication choices are influenced by how we see communication and its connection to human relations. If we think meaning is primarily in the words or symbols we use, then we may see all of communication as primarily a matter of precision or correct grammar. But if we see meaning as created in the relationships between people, then we may see communication as much more than the meaning of words. As we have begun to see, communication is also about attitudes, feelings, and emotions!

# ◆ CHAPTER 2

## ORGANIZATIONAL COMMUNICATION IS ABOUT MESSAGES AND PEOPLE

After reading Chapter 1, you now should appreciate how two-way communication helps people in organizations perform necessary tasks by effectively initiating action through commands and by limiting those actions in clearly prescribed ways through feedback. In addition, this view depicts organizations as the combination of a number of different components, each of which is linked to each other on the basis of some carefully planned and clearly articulated design.

To summarize, the description usually involves three distinct steps:

1. Organizational design begins with an analysis of *goals* and decisions about what goods or services should be produced.

2. *Tasks* are identified in order to produce the desired outcome, and to determine how tasks can be performed most efficiently.

3. Tasks are organized into *structures* and *sequences,* which maximize the total operation.

As you have seen, the command function of communication allows organizational members to transmit information necessary for the rational completion of tasks. Members perform tasks effectively only when they give and receive prompt and accurate feedback, publications, and instructions. Precision and clarity are the hallmarks of this approach to organization and communication.

We will now look at how organizations are designed in ways that require their members to rely on another type of communication—relational communication. In order to better understand the less rational world of relational communication in organizational communication, let's first look at the dual nature of organizations.

# ◆ THE DUAL NATURE OF ORGANIZATIONS

You might have played a game when you were a child where you would whisper a message into the ear of a friend. This friend would then repeat the message to another friend. This process would be repeated down a long line of kids. You might recall that a message such as "The rain in Spain falls mainly on the plain" might end up as "A crane fell in the lane when hit by a plane."

The challenges of organizational communication are similar in principle to this example. "Organizational communication" is not only concerned with formal communication (command) but with informal and less rationally-oriented communication (relational) as well. One way of introducing this discussion is to look at the distinction between vertical and horizontal communication.

## Vertical and Horizontal Communication

Although we will be discussing vertical and horizontal working relationships later in another chapter, it is important to first look at the more "macro" issue of vertical and horizontal communication in organizations. Vertical communication refers to either upward or downward organizational communication. Downward communication consists of management directives or information regarding changes in the work environment. Upward communication consists of feedback from subordinates designed to keep managers in touch with what is happening (e.g., were directives carried out or orders followed?).

Problems with vertical communication are usually associated with questions of formal position and hierarchy. Large organizations tend to have "tall" organizational charts with several managerial layers and numerous positions. Vertical communication is more necessary and efficient under these circumstances. However, dissatisfaction results if people are excluded from these more formal communication channels. It is not surprising, then, that such dissatisfaction often occurs in large organizations, which depend more heavily on complex organizational charts.

Another problem associated with positional differences in "tall" organizations is the tendency of subordinates to be hesitant to pass on negative messages to superiors. As a result of this tendency, known as the MUM Effect, an organization could be on the verge of disaster and top management wouldn't know until it was too late!

---

*As you can see, vertical communication tends to be the arena of the command function of communication.*

---

On the other hand, horizontal communication in organizations flows across individuals and work groups at the same level. While definitely affected by questions of status and position, its primary purpose is to facilitate *coordination*

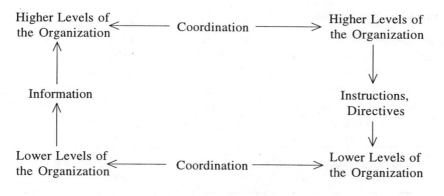

HORIZONTAL

**FIGURE 2.1 VERTICAL AND HORIZONTAL COMMUNICATION**

of efforts among its organizational members. This coordination occurs within a work group or between groups and individuals.

*Horizontal communication tends to be the arena of the relational function of communication.*

Problems with horizontal communication are usually associated with less rational and formal questions of human effort and motivation. Vertical communication can be hampered in organizations not only by issues of formal structure, but also because individuals, departments, or divisions sometimes jealously guard their own territories.

For example, the manager of the eastern division runs down the achievements of the western division by lamenting missed deadlines. Or the secretary of the main office snipes at the mail room supervisor by harping on a lost memo. It is often the case that it is more important for *aggressors* to get at other individuals or groups than it is for their own areas to succeed.

*Dominators* want to run things more than they want to solve problems or communicate effectively. A computer room supervisor may want to take over the entire human resources department so problems in the computer room are never thoroughly discussed until they're big enough to affect the supervisor's personal agenda. The computer room typically teeters on the edge of chaos, but the supervisor gets his promotion—at the cost, of course, of productivity and effective communication.

### Informal Communication

Although discussion of organizational communication can easily be focused on the formal organization, the differences between vertical and horizontal communication show us that there is also an "informal" organization. No company document portrays the informal organization and its communication, as this "organization" is determined by the power, politics, friendship ties, and proximity of organization members.

*The informal organization and its communication are riddled with uncertainties. In other words—human relations!*

For example, the *grapevine* is an informal communication channel that exists in all organizations. The grapevine stems from the need of people to understand what is happening around them. Although the grapevine is surprisingly accurate, its main purpose is to act as an "escape valve" for employee tensions and is usually quite active in organizations undergoing considerable change.

It has been estimated that about 80 percent of the information transmitted through a grapevine is correct. Problems occur, however, because of the 20 percent of grapevine information that is inaccurate and, even if accurate, information may not be understood in context.

The grapevine is the communication channel that carries all *rumors*. As many of us know, it is very difficult to combat rumors. Nevertheless, managers should never forget the grapevine. Managers combat rumors carried by the grapevine by providing accurate information, by challenging the source of a rumor, and by encouraging subordinates to recall facts or experiences of their own that are contrary to the rumor.

### ◆ THE RELATIONAL FUNCTION OF COMMUNICATION

As suggested by the dynamics of horizontal and informal communication and the grapevine, communication in organizations is considerably more than official "commands."

*Organizations are composed of human beings who are involved in interpersonal relationships with other human beings.*

Human organizations are not always rational, carefully planned combinations of interrelated, static components. They are made up of living, thinking, emotional human beings—*actors* who constantly make choices—not inanimate objects of the organization.

---

*Organizations are networks of interdependent human relations.*
*Because people are dynamic, organizations are dynamic.*

---

In other words, communication is also important for *relational* reasons. Instead of being solely command-oriented, communication is a medium of relationships and community. In the relational realm, perceptions and emotions—not tasks, commands, or logical sequences—provide the guidelines within which individuals make decisions about how to act.

For example, uncertainty tends to be the hallmark of relational communication in organizations. Instead of depending on clarity and precision, relational communication accepts the reality of human uncertainty. In fact, relational communication helps people to communicate with others in order to give structure to new and ambiguous situations.

People who understand the importance of relational communication seek out information that will help them gain a perspective on problems. They also seek out support from others, which will confirm or disconfirm their interpretation of the problem and strengthen their commitment to a preferred action. Through communication with other members of the organization, they are able to create a *shared* understanding of what a problem is and how it should be addressed. Thus, not only do they depend on sufficient, relevant, and accurate information, but they act to create a shared perspective as a path to improved decision-making.

Relational communication is a process through which people make sense out of—not control—the actions of other people. It is the medium within which they are able to understand how they coordinate their actions with the actions of others. It emphasizes how human action is contextualized by uncertainty.

---

*Good organizational communication*
*begins at the relational level.*

---

Effective organizational communication begins in the qualities of human relationships. If personal relationships and communication are not effective, then organizational communication—vertical or horizontal communication within an entire organization—also falters.

# ◆ ONE CANNOT *NOT* COMMUNICATE

We think of command communication as being intentional, purposeful, and rationally motivated. In relational communication, we are communicating even though we might not think we are or might not even want to communicate. Take, for example, what we call *nonverbal communication*. As teachers, we often see students sitting in the back of the room with "expressionless" faces, perhaps staring at the front of the room, perhaps staring out the window. Although many of these students might say that they are not communicating with us or other students, they are obviously communicating a great deal—perhaps disinterest, perhaps boredom, perhaps a desire for class to be over as soon as possible. In any event, these students are communicating whether they wish to or not.

---

*As Joseph Devito observes, we cannot NOT communicate.*

---

Nonverbal communication illustrates that communication is inevitable. The issue to be considered in relational communication is how we can exert some positive effect. Although we can make our "commands" clearer and more precise to encourage understanding, we cannot control all aspects of our relational communication, particularly nonverbal elements, but we can have some productive influence. The following examples of nonverbal communication further illustrate the increased complexity of relational communication and the possibilities for positive interactions.

## Body Language (Kinesics)

Body language, or kinesics, includes the whole gamut of nonverbal cues: eye contact, body posture, facial expression, gestures, and body movement. It is a highly speculative field and difficult to define and understand, but there is no question about its importance—the way a message is sent is often more relevant than what is said.

Albert Mehrabian has observed that a significant portion of communication is expressed without words. Much of our meaning is expressed by facial gestures, posture, and vocal intonation and inflection. In fact, it may be a smaller part of communication that is actually verbal.

Judgments from visual cues are often more "valid" to people than judgments from vocal communication. When verbal and nonverbal messages differ, we tend to believe the nonverbal. Judgments from visual cues in the environment are more accurate than are judgments based upon vocal cues.

---

*It is more difficult to control our nonverbal communication.*

---

The importance of nonverbal communication, and kinesics in particular, cannot be overemphasized. Positive nonverbal behaviors and body language have a significant positive affect on perceptions of observers. But while describing "positive" nonverbal behavior in general terms is not difficult, the difficulty lies in being specific about which nonverbal behavior or body movement is effective under particular circumstances.

Take eye contact, for example. Under most circumstances, making eye contact with another is perceived as a positive nonverbal behavior. However, too much eye contact can make another person uneasy. Indeed, to fix someone with a "cold stare" is usually a sign of hostility. In certain cultures, eye contact acceptable by Western standards might be perceived as being rude (for example, in the Japanese culture). The same thing can be said with regard to certain gestures.

Rather than provide you with a list of constructive nonverbal behaviors to be used in all circumstances, we offer some observations, with recommendations. First, it is impossible to avoid communicating through body language. As we observed, one cannot not communicate. Think about it. Nonverbal communication shows us that everything we say or do—or are—sends a message.

Second, never forget that body language, including voice intonation and inflection, plays a very significant role in communication, sometimes even more important than the words that are actually spoken. Managers should understand that appropriate nonverbal communication is embedded in context. Above all, the key to effective nonverbal communication is sensitivity to one's environment and relationships.

Consequently, you might want to occasionally conduct a periodic, personal sensitivity audit to ascertain what your nonverbal communication might be saying to others. For example, when speaking, notice if your audience is fidgeting or looking bored. Is the audience nodding with approval? What's going on? In the process of conducting this sensitivity audit, consider whether your verbal and nonverbal communication is congruent. Work toward congruence between verbal and nonverbal communication for the purpose of clarifying communication.

Also, you can observe the nonverbal communication of others. Be sure to use active listening skills to "check out" nonverbal cues emanating from those around you. For example, if a person with whom you are communicating loudly and obviously yawns, don't get angry. Instead, check out the yawn. You might observe, "Ralph, it looks like you're bored with what I'm saying." Ralph can then respond by telling you that he stayed up all night in anticipation of your meeting. Ralph isn't bored, he's tired!

**Spatial Relations (Proxemics)**

Another area of nonverbal communication that is important for relational communication is spatial relations, or proxemics, the study of the way people use space. The anthropologist Edward T. Hall defined four distinct distances of which people are aware: intimate, personal, social, and public distances. These "distances" range from skin contact up to 18 inches for intimate encounters to 12 feet and beyond for public distance.

The major implication of proxemics is to be mindful of the effect personal distance has upon those around you. Most communication in organizational meetings uses "social distance," which ranges from four to 12 feet. "Personal distance," 18 inches to four feet, is often employed in interpersonal communication.

As with other nonverbal communication, it is difficult to control or set rules for maintaining personal space. The effect of personal distance should be factored into the "sensitivity audit" described previously (e.g., "Am I too close? Should I back off? Is "personal distance" appropriate in this setting with this person?").

A related concern pertains to "touch." Touching, outside of incidental contact and handshakes (as part of a mutually understood greeting ritual), is always intimate. Sometimes it is appropriate to slap another on the back or touch an arm to emphasize a point. For the most part, however, at least in Western culture, managers should avoid extensive touching as part of their interpersonal communication repertoire.

Another application of proxemics concerns open versus closed office design. An office with an open design typically has the desk and chairs aligned so that there are no physical barriers between those sitting in the office. Conversely, offices with closed designs typically place a desk or other office furniture between people.

People feel more welcome and comfortable in offices with an open design compared to offices with closed designs. Also, people tend to view the occupants of offices with an open design as being friendlier and more helpful. Consequently, an open office design should be used by people in the helping professions, such as counselors and professors. The question of whether this statement extends to people in other organizational settings is debatable. We tend to favor open office design because such a design facilitates relational communication.

## Temporal Relations (Chronemics)

An important but often overlooked element of nonverbal communication is the use of time, or chronemics. The importance of time in organizational communication can be seen everywhere. We set dates for the completion of projects, schedule meetings, and negotiate working hours—including coffee and lunch breaks.

*The employee who is frequently late for work communicates
disorganization, disinterest, and disrespect
to co-workers and managers.*

Most organizations develop definite standards for the use of time. It is usually expected that employees never arrive late for a meeting or an appointment with a supervisor, but it is sometimes acceptable for a manager to arrive late or keep an employee waiting. Although such behavior is not effective relational communication, it is an example of important organizational information.

We will discuss the importance of time in organizational communication in a later chapter on e-mail, or "online" communication. It is sufficient to say at this point that attitudes toward time are communicated by the ways individuals deal with it.

## ◆  PRACTICING RELATIONAL COMMUNICATION SKILLS

As you may now understand, the purpose of organizational communication is two-fold:

1.  To transmit messages as clearly and accurately as possible in order to achieve productive levels of understanding, and

2.  To maintain positive relationships with your co-workers.

Following are a few concluding reminders for improving your relational communication:

1.  *Appreciate that "one cannot not communicate."* It is pervasive, including all nonverbal and written, as well as oral, behaviors that others always interpret as communication.

2.  *Watch your nonverbal communication.* Check out discrepancies perceived in the verbal and nonverbal communication of others. Also, check out nonverbal cues of others whenever there are doubts or questions with regard to meaning. Watch your body language. Orient body and face to indicate a favorable attitude toward the individual. Display a desire to include the other person in communication. Be mindful of the importance of personal space. Do not inappropriately violate the personal space of others. Use an open office design intended to facilitate interpersonal communication with others. And watch the time—failure to observe the standards communicates

nonverbal messages that can reduce your chance for success in the organization.

3. *Don't forget the grapevine!* Combat rumors carried by the grapevine by providing accurate information, challenging the source of a rumor, and encouraging subordinates to recall facts or experiences of their own that are contrary to the rumor. Be sure to use credible sources of information in your own communication—sources that employees will believe. Be sure to answer questions directly and specifically whenever possible and admit uncertainty when impossible, but explain the causes of the uncertainty. Try to involve employees in the problem-solving process as much as possible.

# ◆ CHAPTER 3
## ORGANIZATIONAL COMMUNICATION IS ABOUT CHOICE

As Chapters 1 and 2 have emphasized, effective organizational communication involves both command and relational skills. As such, "problems" with organizational communication are normal because communication involves people, and people are often imprecise, unclear, and unpredictable.

*Effective communicators understand that communication is always a matter of coping with the uncertainties and ambiguities of other people in the organization.*

This chapter suggests that many of the communication frustrations that we experience day-to-day in organizations result from how we *perceive* communication and its relationship to the human factor. Perceptions direct our communication behaviors. For example, if we assume that meaning is primarily in the words or symbols we use, then we see communication as primarily a matter of precision or correct grammar. We may be frustrated with the uncertainties of human relations, but if we assume meaning is created in the interaction between people, then we see communication as more than the meaning of words. It includes attitudes, feelings, and emotions. We can then be more prepared to cope with the ambiguities of human relations.

*We choose to be either impersonal or interpersonal in our communication, but we need to aware of how choice plays a part in our communication behavior.*

Choice is always a part of human communication. We stress the idea in this chapter because we have had many students come into our classes believing that circumstances and other people force them to communicate one way or another. They don't think they have choices when it comes to communication.

We believe that we always have choices—whether to react negatively or respond thoughtfully to things that happen to us and to what other people say. The hope is that this empowering idea will influence your future communication encounters in your organization.

# ◆ MUTATING OUR METAPHORS

Developing effective choices in communication involves looking at how we perceive or "see" communication. For example, people who see communication as "debate" or "performance" may limit their choices in such a way as to encourage negative arguments or stagefright. If you feel you're in a "debate," you naturally try to "win," don't you? Likewise, isn't it natural to have stagefright if you feel like you're on a stage "performing"?

Communication does not have to be seen either as a debate or a performance. Many people try to see communication in other ways—such as a "conversation," for example. They understand that seeing communication as a conversation puts our choices into a much different perspective. People don't have to "win" conversations or "act" for the sake of conversational partners, do they? Well, maybe, but people are less inclined to debate or perform if communication feels more like a conversation and less like a debate or performance.

The organizational theorist Karl Weick describes how our communication behavior is based on *guiding metaphors* and uses the phrase "mutate your metaphors" to describe the skill of changing how one sees communication. In Weick's sense, "mutate" means change and "metaphor" means the major image we carry around in our hearts and minds to describe communication.

As Weick points out, guiding metaphors may not be at the conscious level and effort is required to bring them to awareness. To illustrate this, Ken does a classroom activity where he draws a chalk line on the board that represents what we typically identify as a "bird" or "seagull." He then asks the class, "What do you see?" Students immediately respond, "Bird!" "Seagull!" Ken then asks again, "What do you see?" For a moment, students look confused, but then a hearty soul joins the game and hollers, "Mountains!" Another yells, "A sideways number three?" "Eyebrows!" The responses mount until they sometimes reach 15 or 20. (Ken always knows when the students are fully in the game and actively playing with mutating their metaphors. At that point, someone screams out a part of the human anatomy.)

The awareness activity shows that we don't always consciously know that we see things one way or another, but that we can change our perceptions if we are encouraged to try. This idea is important because the misuse of metaphors leads to personal and professional problems.

---

*We act on our guiding metaphors, so it is important that we*
*analyze them and their possible consequences.*

---

Metaphors can be deeply flawed. If a metaphor communicates a narrow, shallow view of a person or organization, it leads to the inability to articulate a careful analysis of problems and to the alienation of people. For example, seeing communication as "war" distorts and limits thoughtful responses. If we expect a war, we line up all of our communication "weapons" and "attack" our "opponent." We are definitely not in the state of mind to be open to what the other person has to say or to let down our defenses and disclose some personal information.

Common sports metaphors, along with other outmoded images—military and cowboy—can become obsessive. People and organizations lose the capacity to think and act appropriately because they are trapped subconsciously in an irrelevant and inappropriate system of thought and communication.

As a management device, metaphors can be helpful or they can be rooted in an irrelevant past. In meetings and memos, companies often refer to their organizations as "protective families." Obviously, the metaphor communicates a sense of belonging and commitment, but it also communicates the idea that since you do not fire your kids, you do not terminate employees. This metaphor has put many organizations in very challenging positions during a time of "downsizing."

Metaphors are useful for clarifying complex situations by drawing on simpler and less ambiguous images of life. The way we talk and write frames the way we look at the world and shapes the way we think. But as Weick observes, a person needs to consciously choose when it is useful to see communication in another way. We need to mutate our metaphors and begin seeing communication in ways more appropriate to the specific organization and situation. The next section will discuss an approach for doing this with our own communication.

## Choosing How to Communicate

One way that we mutate our metaphors and increase our sense of choice about organizational communication is by expanding our own definition of "interpersonal communication." As a metaphor for understanding communication, interpersonal communication is considered by many people to be limited to what happens between *two* people—husband-wife, parent-child, employer-employee—in mostly face-to-face situations.

But situations are only one way of seeing interpersonal communication. "Interpersonal" can also be seen as the label for a *type* or *quality* of communication that can be present in a variety of situations with a lot of different people. As a quality, interpersonal communication can happen in various organizational situations—on the phone, over the computer, in writing, in committees or other groups, and even in public presentation situations.

How can we mutate our metaphor and begin to think of interpersonal as a quality of communication? John Stewart—professor, mentor, and friend—offers the idea of an *Interpersonal–Impersonal Continuum*. This visual aid or metaphor points to the many possibilities for interpersonal communication. It emphasizes that interpersonal communication is not restricted to situations like the number of people or face-to-face contact, but is a choice that we can make in a variety of situations.

Imagine the continuum:

INTERPERSONAL————————————IMPERSONAL

The Continuum works by placing various communication situations somewhere on the quality spectrum. It is no longer a question of either impersonal or interpersonal communication, but of shades or degrees. We move left or right along the Continuum depending on our choice to be more or less interpersonal in any particular situation.

---

*No matter what the situation, the* Interpersonal–Impersonal
Continuum *assumes that we have a choice*
*to be more or less interpersonal.*

---

But on what does the choice depend? How do we know if we want our communication to be more or less interpersonal? What are the specific qualities at each end of the Continuum?

Stewart suggests that there are three things that help us make the choice to be more or less interpersonal in our communication situations, all recognizing that communication is dealing with people: 1) We focus on what makes the other person unique. 2) We respect each person's ability to think and make choices. 3) We pay attention to relevant feelings and to the whole human being.

*First, humans are unique; they are not interchangeable.* An object can be the same as any other object. For example, if we want to put new batteries into our radio so that we can listen to the baseball game, any AA batteries will work, just as any brand computer disk can be properly formatted to work in the computers that we used to write this chapter.

People are never interchangeable. They can be treated that way, but even identical twins are different from each other in many ways. For example, Ken has a best friend named Chad who has an identical twin brother, Phil. Although Ken doesn't know Phil that well, he does recognize how Chad and Phil are very different. It is apparent that they differ in personal styles and tastes, religious preferences, and political views. While they share important experiences and many similar traits, there is only one of each of them. They are each unique.

*Second, humans can think.* They are capable of making choices. If we avoid the arguments over artificial intelligence, we can say that objects don't think like humans do (for the time being). That's because objects can only be chosen, they cannot choose. We turn on our computers. We initiate action. A computer can seem to operate on its own, but it continues to be dependent on choices initiated from the outside.

(This second point needs elaboration. Often the "physically challenged" are treated like objects because they don't appear capable of initiating actions, but there's a difference between the *movements* of objects and the *actions* of people. While movements are fundamentally reflexive in nature, actions are reflective. Even though people can be limited in movement, they are still capable of initiating actions. People are reflective. So the issue is not whether the physically challenged are able to act, but what are the means to communicate those thoughts and actions.)

*Third, humans have feelings.* This probably distinguishes us from objects more than anything else. For example, if you kick a rock, you could probably predict what would happen. If you had information on such things as force, velocity, momentum, and energy, you might even be able to predict exactly where the rock would end up after you kicked it

Now try kicking a person. What will be the human reaction? Will the person cry, look surprised, get angry, or kick you back? You take your chances with the human factor because emotions and feelings can't be measured and calculated. Sure, we measure brain waves, heart rate, pulse, respiration—but that's not the whole person. How people react emotionally to the experiences of their lives and to events continues to be unmeasurable.

On the other hand, if we need our communication to be more efficient, i.e., impersonal, there are three things that help us do that: 1) We focus on the general characteristics of people. 2) We ignore the issue of thinking and choice. 3) We stay away from emotions.

For example, when I'm talking with a bank teller—a situation where there's just the two of us in a face-to-face encounter (normally what we would think of as an "interpersonal" situation)—the Continuum opens up the possibility that our communication can still be on the impersonal end of the scale. Neither we nor the bank teller want to hold up a long line while we have a personal chat about uniqueness, feelings, and choice.

---

*Two people in a face-to-face situation does not mean that communication is or needs to be interpersonal.*

---

Likewise, when we are talking with an entire class of 30 students in a one-to-many situation, the Continuum opens up the possibility that our communication can still be interpersonal. The continuum simply shows that the difference is in the quality of communication, not in the situation. Even in large groups, we can treat people interpersonally by learning their names, encouraging them to ask questions, and responding to nonverbal behaviors.

Again, the point is not that "impersonal" communication is always inappropriate. Because of expectations, time constraints, or a multitude of other factors, it is sometimes the only way to deal efficiently with a situation. The point is that although there are no strict rules or formulas for making these kinds of communication decisions, there are guidelines that help us to make effective choices as communicators.

It is always our choice to be more interpersonal, even in such unexpected organizational settings as speaking to a large group or interacting over a computer.

**The Spiritual Child**

But why choose to be interpersonal? It makes sense to be impersonal when we want to be more efficient. But what is the major reason to be interpersonal?

First, as we already have pointed out, interpersonal or relational communication is a source of important information. While it may not get a specific message delivered or task completed, it gives us a sense of other people's perceptions and emotions. It also helps us to develop a perspective on problems and issues.

Second, interpersonal communication is about *person-building*.

"Person-building" is the idea that the quality of each person's life is a result of the quality of the communication he or she experiences. While communication can be a "tool" to accomplish certain tasks, such as "commands," it also affects who we are as people. For example, any parent knows that there is a big difference between *what* you say to a child (the tool part) and *how* you say it (the person-building part). You can say things such as "Of course I love you" in two very different ways—one tells the child to be reassured and that he or she is worthy of love; the other "says" quite the opposite with sarcasm or conflicting nonverbals (the double-bind), confusing the child and manipulating his or her emotions.

The *"spiritual child"* metaphor symbolizes how communication is a person-building process where both parties are responsible for creating and maintaining a positive relationship. Stewart observes that whenever we encounter someone, the two of us together create a spiritual child—our relationship. Unlike the creation of physical children, there are no contraceptives available for spiritual children; when two people meet, they always create a relationship of some sort. And unlike physical children, the spiritual child lives as long as at least one person lives. We never stop knowing someone.

Consequently, if the spiritual child is born in encounters characterized by manipulation, deceit, and exploitation, it will be deformed and ugly. If the negative encounters continue, the child will never be healthy. A spiritual child can be nurtured back to health, but it takes a heavy commitment from both "parents" to change how they communicate. An open and caring communication atmosphere helps the child grow healthy and strong.

The spiritual child is useful for visualizing how communication "builds people." Like a child, communication is never of either "parent," but the result of the meeting and contact of two people. Most importantly, like the spiritual child who is "born" whenever two people meet, communication always results in a new person emerging from human contact. Communication continually changes us—constantly forming the people we are and the people we will become. Whenever we communicate, we "fuse" our horizon of experience with another person's and come away a "new" person, because we come away with a new understanding.

---

*We become different people whenever we communicate.*
*Communication is a form of "re-creation."*

---

The metaphors of person-building and the spiritual child also highlight the central importance of communication in organizations and human relations. They suggest that organizations, as well as individuals, have a role to play in helping their members to become more productive people.

## ◆ COMMUNICATION CLIMATES

Although it is obvious that communication affects the self-esteem of children and the kind of people they become, it is not always obvious that the same principles apply to working adults. As members of organizations, the question becomes: "Why should organizations be concerned about the kind of persons they are helping to create?"

Organizational scholars like Charles Conrad tell us that productivity and *job satisfaction* are related. The question of how they are related is still up in the air, but experience tells us that low job satisfaction leads to absenteeism, voluntary turnover, and low productivity.

Studies from between 1927 and 1932 at the Hawthorne Plant of the Western Electric Company in Cicero, Illinois, also suggest that employees who are involved in a friendly, relaxed, and congenial work group with supervisors who listen to them, are concerned about their needs, and are supportive, are more productive than other employees, even when other working conditions are not particularly favorable. (Although the studies had some perplexing results, increases in productivity that result from changes in working conditions, and getting feedback from employees on the changes, are now often referred to as the Hawthorne effect.)

In addition, employee satisfaction with social and interpersonal relationships with their peers significantly influences their productivity, and employees feel substantial pressure from their peers to conform to the norms of their work group.

*It seems apparent that interpersonal communication and
person-building are important factors in job satisfaction.*

So now the question changes: How can organizations affect the kind of persons they are helping to create? Other research suggests that there are three things organizations can do to emphasize positive person-building and increase job satisfaction.

First, organizations can recognize that their employees are unique by carefully designing jobs that communicate to employees that jobs fit personal and unique characteristics and skills. In other words, a good way for organizations to view satisfaction and productivity is as outcomes of employee–job interaction.

Too frequently, organizations do not consider the impact of *job design* on employee satisfaction. Jobs are often designed from a technical and efficiency perspective and little attention is given to how the job fits the person. For example, Richard Hackman and Greg Oldman tell us that if an individual employee has high growth needs, then that person would probably fit a job with a high degree of skills variety, task identity, task significance, autonomy, and feedback.

Organizations need to take the unique growth needs of employees into account when designing or redesigning work (with the understanding that job design is most likely to be successful for jobs that can be successfully modified within the context of the organization, for jobs that do not fit employee growth needs, and in situations where managers and employees accept job design as a method for making work more satisfying).

Second, organizations can recognize that their employees are thinkers and give them tasks complex enough to challenge them, but simple enough to accomplish. If a job is too complex, it is frustrating and not satisfying. If it is too simple, it is boring. Consequently, successfully challenging an employee requires a high level of open communication and feedback among supervisors and their subordinates.

Third, organizations can develop the "whole" employee by establishing a positive overall *communication climate*. A communication climate serves as a frame of reference for employee activities and therefore shapes individual expectancies, attitudes, feelings, and behaviors. Through these kinds of effects, communication climates influence organizational outcomes, such as productivity and satisfaction.

It is important to note that communication climates arise from and are sustained by organizational practices. Structural and contextual factors influence communication climates, but their effects are mediated by the actual communication practices of organizational members. As such, communication climates are not static, but constantly in the process of change and development.

One researcher who has studied the concept of climate extensively is W. Charles Redding. He identifies five components that, taken together, drive effective organizational practices and positive communication climates.

They are:

1. The degree to which management communication is *supportive* of its employees' efforts.

2. The extent that communication permits *participative decision-making*.

3. The degree of *trust* employees have in management.

4. The amount of *open communication*.

5. The degree to which an organization communicates *high performance goals*.

One crucial area of organizational practice and communication climate is the quality of *superior–subordinate communication*. No relationship is more central to the effective performance of an organization than that between superior and subordinate. The behavior and performance of individuals, groups, and entire organizations depend critically on the success with which these interactions are managed.

Supportive communication and prompt and accurate performance feedback from supervisors are crucial for increased satisfaction and performance. Except for the necessary security information, employees should have relatively easy access to information that relates directly to their immediate jobs, that affects their abilities to coordinate their work with other employees, and that deals broadly with organizational goals.

Likewise, supervisors must also receive timely and accurate feedback about their subordinates' performance. Employees from each level in the organization should listen with open minds to suggestions or reports of problems made by employees at each subordinate level in the organization. Information from subordinates should be viewed as important enough to be acted upon.

Frederick Jablin concludes that there are three general factors that have a marked influence on the success of communication between superior and subordinate:

First, *power* is an influence over the actions of another person or group. Subordinates who perceive their superiors as having substantial upward influence on their own superiors are more satisfied with those superiors and tend to communicate more frequently with them.

Second, *trust* mediates the relationship between communication openness and effectiveness. When a great deal of trust exists between subordinate and superior, communication openness can have a positive effect on communication effectiveness.

Third, the *information gap* between superior and subordinate affects effective communication. Too wide a gap will distort communication and make it less effective, but too thin a gap might be harmful in terms of decreasing the diversity of information and various interpretations of issues.

# ◆ DEVELOPING INTERPERSONAL COMPETENCE

As this chapter has outlined, the way our day-to-day communication functions in organizations is partly a result of how we *perceive* communication and its relationship to the human factor.

*Choice-making is a necessary part of human communication
and offers a way for responding to various communication
challenges and situations, but appropriate choices depend on
the ability to see communication situations in a variety of ways.*

Changing the guiding metaphors we use for clarifying complex communication situations helps to reveal communication choices. What might have been considered an impersonal setting is reframed to have many interpersonal possibilities. An interaction with another employee that was only seen as a phase of task completion becomes an opportunity to affect the quality of someone's life, including your own.

*Organizations can recognize their employees as whole
and unique human beings by establishing a
positive overall communication climate.*

Overall, this chapter has reinforced the idea that effective organizational communication is two-fold: the ability to transmit messages clearly and accurately *and* the ability to maintain positive relationships with co-workers. In fact, the chapter may have tilted the balance between these two functions a little more to the relational side. In some ways, it suggests that, as the German philosopher Karl Jaspers put it, our "supreme achievement in the world is communication from personality to personality."

*More than merely sending messages or accomplishing tasks,
interpersonal communication builds positive self-esteems,
effective working relationships, and productive organizations.*

The next chapter introduces a model for developing communication competence in organizations, but we preview the process here by concluding with a few reminders for improving interpersonal communication skills:

1. *Watch your own communication metaphors.* Effectiveness in today's work world must begin with a broader, more realistic picture of the people and the communication that makes up contemporary organizations.

2. *Build choice into your communication behaviors.* People make choices about how to communicate within organizations defined by past choices, perceptions of the current situation, and the ability to see communication situations differently. Assume that you have choices when it comes to communication and look for possibilities.

3. *Choose to be interpersonal in appropriate situations.* Look for opportunities to treat co-workers as unique, feeling, and thinking human beings. Don't ignore the fact that even a simple hello in the hallway helps to build self-esteems, working relationships, and positive communication climates.

4. *Actively contribute to a positive communication climate.* When appropriate, use supportive communication to encourage democratic decision-making and to build collective trust. Practice open communication while setting high standards.

# ◆ CHAPTER 4
## ORGANIZATIONAL COMMUNICATION AND INDIVIDUAL COMPETENCE

As Chapter 3 emphasized, many of our day-to-day communication activities in organizations are influenced by how we perceive communication and its role in our working relationships.

---

*Perceptions of people and communication influence our actual communication practices.*

---

In addition, choice is a necessary part of human communication. We always have choice in communication—whether to react negatively or respond thoughtfully to things that happen to us and to what other people say. Consequently, our perceptions of communication affect our ability to make effective choices.

In this chapter, we move beyond perception and concentrate on an approach for developing practical communication competence in organizations. The effectiveness of any organization depends to a great extent on the communication knowledge and performance of its members. Individuals and groups carry out various roles and functions in the organizing process. Whether a person is a manager, supervisor, employee, or consultant, there is a need for competent communication.

---

*The needs of contemporary organizations are producing an enlarging role for competent communicators.*

---

This chapter identifies a set of communication competencies that serve to synthesize some of the issues already raised in this book, and to align those issues with specific recommendations from the Secretary of Labor's Commission on Achieving Necessary Skills (SCANS) in the workplace. It then presents an integrative model of communication competence that offers an individual approach for enhancing communication skills, stressing competence as a balance between thought and action. The model is based on the assumption that it is not enough just to know what your communication options are. You must "try on the behaviors" in real organizational situations. Following that are some guidelines for planning your own program for developing communication competence.

## ◆ THE COMMUNICATION DEMANDS OF ORGANIZATIONS

So far, this book has concentrated more on "macro-oriented" issues of communication functions in organizations and on the importance of choice in communication behaviors and communication climates. It is now time to show how those larger issues can be translated into the "micro-skills" of individuals who want to communicate better in their organizations.

As a way to begin, we turn to a report by the Secretary of Labor's Commission on Achieving Necessary Skills. SCANS was asked to examine the level of skills required to succeed in the workplace. In carrying out this charge, the Commission defined the skills needed for employment.

---

*The SCANS message to us is crucial: Good jobs will increasingly depend on people who are competent at communication skills.*

---

SCANS information suggests that what we call *workplace know-how* is essentially skills in command and relational communication as discussed in previous chapters. This know-how has two main elements: competencies (knowledge areas) and foundations (skills). The report identifies three "competencies" that are directly related to organizational communication: information (command), interpersonal (relational), and systems (climate)

The *informational competency* is the knowledge and skill to acquire and use organizational information. We might call this the "command competency." It includes four attributes of effective command communication:

- Acquires and evaluates information

- Organizes and maintains information

- Interprets and communicates information

- Uses information technology to process information

The *interpersonal competency* is the knowledge and skill to work with other organizational members. We could call this the "relational competency." It emphasizes seven areas of relational communication:

- *Participates as member of a team*—contributes to effective group communication.

- *Teaches others new skills*—communicates knowledge and skills to others.

- *Serves clients and customers*—communicates in a way to satisfy product and process expectations.

- *Exercises leadership*—communicates ideas to make position responsive, persuades and convinces others, responsibly challenges existing procedures and policies.

- *Negotiates*—works with others toward agreements involving exchange of resources, communicates through conflict and divergent interests.

- *Works with diversity*—communicates well with men and women from diverse backgrounds.

The *systems competency* is the knowledge and skill to understand complex organizational interrelationships. We might call this the "climate competency." It includes both command and relational elements, stressing the systematic dynamic of change and development that exists among people, information, and technology:

- *Understands systems*—knows how social, organizational, and technological systems function and communicates effectively with them.

- *Evaluates performance*—evaluates trends and impacts on system operations and responds to system dynamics.

- *Improves and designs systems*—suggests changes to existing systems and develops new and alternative systems to improve performance and productivity.

The SCANS competencies serve to synthesize a number of organizational communication issues, including many that you find discussed in this book. They are an "organizing device" for making sense of organizational communication and for putting the information in this book into perspective.

But the SCANS competencies also lead the way to an individual approach to skills development. In the next section, we offer a model of communication competence that suggests individuals must learn to assess their own communication proficiency and plan their own communication development.

## ◆ AN INDIVIDUAL APPROACH FOR DEVELOPING COMMUNICATION COMPETENCE

As a practical point, it is helpful to look at a model of developing communication competence based on learning relevant to the individual (Table 4.1). The ideas of people like Jerome Bruner, R.R. Allen, and Kenneth L. Brown have contributed to a four-stage model of communication competence in which the employee and manager learns from *watching, choosing, doing,* and *reflecting.*

The individual approach of the model recognizes that, unfortunately, the professional development of communication competence remains a haphazard process and individuals must take responsibility for their own improvement. In addition, most workshops, experiences, and courses for developing communication skills have focused on supplying "rules" that treat communication behavior as a logical equation—a sort of "If/Then" procedure. They ignore the role of communication choice.

The communication competence model is quite different. It doesn't present ideas in terms of "rules." It prefers students to think of "guidelines" for communication behavior. Guidelines leave room for individual reflection and choice. No two communication situations are ever alike, so no one formula will always work.

## TABLE 4.1 COMMUNICATION COMPETENCE MODEL

1. *Observing a Variety of Communication Acts*
   To be effective communicators, organizational members must be flexible actors, capable of performing a wide range of communication acts as required by the people, settings, and tasks of the organization. The first element of competence is observing the communication performance of others. By watching others, communicators begin to build a list or "repertoire" of available communication acts.

2. *Choosing an Appropriate Communication Act*
   Communication competence is based on the appropriateness of what people say, given consideration to other people, time, place, subject matter, and the goal or purpose of the situation.

3. *Implementing a Communication Act*
   Once people have made an appropriate communication choice for a particular situation, they must "try on the behavior" by actually demonstrating their ability to carry their choice into action.

4. *Judging the Communication Act*
   People cannot depend on rules to communicate effectively, but must reflect on their own communication behavior and evaluate communication acts in terms of satisfaction to themselves and others.

*The key to effective communication skills is not reactions based
on rules, but choices based on reflection.*

To function effectively as competent communicators in organizations, we must have continuing experiences by which we learn to reflect on our own actions. Based on the assumption that communication competence is a dynamic learning experience involving individual reflection, the model characterizes competence with four elements:

### First, Competence Is Variable

An individual does not simply possess communication competence. Rather, competence is a matter of degree. A member of an organization is never entirely competent or incompetent, but one may be more or less so. Individuals vary in their competence level from moment to moment and from situation to situation. Consequently, we learn from each other. We learn to be more competent communicators if we make it a point to observe the communication behaviors of others. Communication competence requires an openness to learn from others and a willingness to risk new situations.

*Communication competence is never something that is
possessed. It is always relative to our working relationships.*

### Second, Competence Is Situational

Competence is not a cross-situational trait, but means recognizing the *appropriateness* of a specific communication act in relation to some specific situation. For example, the aggressive defense of one's ideas may not be appropriate in one organizational setting, but perfectly appropriate in another. You don't defend your ideas and attack another's if you are in a brainstorming session. Brainstorming's purpose is to encourage the creation of many different ideas. Aggressive evaluation of ideas destroys the safe environment of brainstorming that permits people to take intellectual risks.

Only when the aggressive defense of ideas is deemed appropriate will such communication behavior be seen as competent. For example, after a few ideas have been selected as possible solutions to a problem, then is the right time for aggressive judgment. If an idea cannot be defended, it may not have "cash value."

Communication competence is largely a function of the particular relationship and situation. Someone judged highly competent in one relationship or situation may be incompetent in another. As many people know, Thomas Paine was extremely competent at communicating the need for the American Revolution, but communicating through the specific details of creating a new government bored him. This is why flexibility and adaptability are frequently associated with communication competence.

---

*Communication competence is about people who adapt well to the situational contingencies of communication and who are more often perceived as competent than those who do not.*

---

### Third, Competence Is Functional

To be competent is to accomplish things with your communication. People must "do" something with their communication that is seen as valuable by other people or by themselves. Competent communicators need to have knowledge and skill. *Knowledge* is the sense of how to communicate in an appropriate way, and *skill* is the ability to actually communicate.

---

*Communication competence is not just about "knowing" skills; it's about the willingness to apply skills to appropriate situations.*

---

### Fourth, Competence Is Reflective

What is evaluated in establishing an individual's communication competence? The most important criterion is *satisfaction*. How satisfying is the outcome of the communication response? Can the result or outcome of the communication act be deemed satisfactory in terms of how well it worked in a particular situation?

In addition, the perceived results of an interaction by other people need to be important elements in whether an individual judges a communication act to be satisfactory. The outcome of a communication act is always a function of a particular relationship. How satisfactory the result of a communication interaction is seen to represent depends largely on the expectations of that relationship.

---

*Communication competence is the ability to reflect on the satisfaction of past communication experiences in relational terms and to plan changes for the future.*

---

As an individual, group leader, or organizational manager, it is necessary not only to understand the change process when it comes to communication, but also to plan the process of change. The communication competence model helps you to understand the process of improving your organizational communication skills.

The following section provides a number of guidelines for improving personal competence.

**GUIDELINES FOR PLANNING
COMMUNICATION COMPETENCE**

Individual challenges to improving communication competence will be less intense when those who are affected plan the change. This is done most effectively by having some guidelines for the actual planning. In addition, besides helping people to understand the "how" of improving communication, guidelines stimulate many other good ideas.

In 1946, Kurt Lewin described change as a three-step process, requiring: 1) "unfreezing" old behaviors through training, 2) "moving" toward effective new behavior by becoming a change agent, and 3) "refreezing" new behaviors through organizational reinforcements.

The following guidelines are suggested to help you begin the process of "unfreezing" old communication behaviors and planning for improved communication skills. The guidelines are all forms of "training," but they also serve as a catalyst for creating your own ideas and transforming yourself into a personal "change agent." By incorporating these guidelines into your own communication values and behaviors, you might be in the position to affect your organization's communication climate and help "refreeze" a new set of communication standards.

Some guidelines for planning this process are:

1. *Getting feedback.* A basic strategy for developing communication competence, and a great source of professional growth, is the practice of gathering feedback information from those you work with and are trying to serve. You should develop some type of communication feedback tool as part of as many interactions as possible.

   There is no better way to build an effective working relationship, as well as to learn about your own communication performance, than to review "how" things are going. For example, we suggest that work teams donate time at the end of every session to how the team process went. Five minutes of discussion at the end of a meeting about the strengths and weaknesses of that day's group process contributes to the group effort, helps to organize and maintain information, and modifies the existing group process in order to improve team performance.

2. *Mentoring relationships.* Another great source of support and stimulus to a communicator's professional growth is to team with a colleague either as a peer or apprentice. A mentoring relationship requires planning together, which means sharing, testing, modifying, defending, and articulating values, concepts, rationale, designs, and techniques. There is the opportunity to observe the communication performance of someone you respect, elicit feedback in a safe environment about your own communication performance, debrief each other, and learn from the shared experience.

3. *Self-documentation.* It is important for persons interested in improving their communication to document what they do as communicators. Documentation is a means for collecting the list of communication responses that make up your repertoire of knowledge and skills. Logs, journals, and diaries are effective ways for recording your observations and judgments. They help you learn new communication skills and acquire and evaluate new information.

    Self-documentation is also the basis of setting communication goals. It is essential that a professional person have clearly developed targets for improving communication competence. A number of communication inventories and self-help materials are available to aid in a process that provides the direction and integration of the various activities in which one engages for communication improvement.

4. *Professional development.* Some of the most interesting and supportive professional opportunities for increasing communication competence come from being an active member of a professional association. It helps communication growth to be affiliated with one or more such groups and to participate in their meetings. It offers more opportunities for participating as a team member and for exercising leadership.

5. *Sharing experiences with co-workers.* Most of us are inhibited in expressing curiosity about what our co-workers do and how they do it. However, this curiosity reflects a desire to learn, which can be very rewarding to others as well as to yourself. The exchange of concrete experiences of communication failure and success is probably the most unused resource for enhancing communication competence.

6. *Risking new learning opportunities.* The activities of this course you are enrolled in right now respond to many of the guidelines already mentioned. But, more than anything, your participation in the course shows that you are already responding to this guideline—you are willing to risk new learning opportunities. Coming back to school is not always easy. There are concerns about money, work obligations, and family responsibilities. You might wonder if you are cut out to be a "student." Do you have the skills? Will education have a positive impact on your life?

    You already know that while new learning opportunities are a risk to self-esteem, tight schedules, and other responsibilities, they also provide a rich menu of growth stimulation, knowledge, and skills. They offer communication experience with men and women from diverse backgrounds. They help us acquire and use information. It's important to risk participation in opportunities for professional development and learning.

7. *Reading programs.* It is essential to develop a reading program to improve communication competence. This would not only include college texts, articles, and research papers, but also contemporary journals, papers, and

magazines. The challenge is in developing the self-discipline to set aside a regular time period for reading about communication.

Of course, your program has already begun. This text offers information in many new areas of communication skill development, such as working relationships, communication climates, teamwork, listening, communicating through conflict, e-mail communication, and constructive feedback. The other parts of your challenge are to find ways to apply the information in this text to real communication situations and to go beyond the confines of the book and create a reading program for lifelong learning.

## ◆ CONCLUSION

The development of communication competence takes many different forms. It may be formal, with readings, assignments, and activities fully written, including specifications and deadlines for their completion, or it may be informal and completely within the work experience of a person.

The nature of the situation determines the formality, the detail, the responsibility, and the methods of planning your communication development. Whatever the nature of the situation, it is generally agreed that a plan is a most important part of the process. The only link between a professional desire to improve your communication and its realization is the blueprint showing the parts needed, how they are put together, and the order in which to handle them.

This chapter has offered such a blueprint. The communication competence model provides a way for making sense of our communication experiences and for enhancing our own communication skills. It does not depend on rules, but on the ability of people to observe the communication behaviors in their own organizations and to reflect on their own actions.

As we hope you see by this point, the purpose of the communication competence model is two-fold:

1. To offer guidelines for improving your communication.

2. To encourage the ability to make communication choices.

Following are a few suggestions for using the model to get the most out of the rest of this book:

1. *Identify specific skills in the book that you would like to add to your own repertoire of communication acts.* Reading this book should not be a passive process where you are the recipient of someone else's meaning. Reading is an active and selective process. To learn how to become a competent communicator in an organization, you must actively identify and select the skills you need.

2. *Decide whether a specific skill is appropriate to your situation.* The active learner in all aspects of understanding is that person who pays attention to the information that is most relevant to his or her own needs. Learning to be a competent communicator is about application of ideas for your own purposes. Application can begin with reading. As you read this book, reflect on whether the ideas apply to your own working relationships.

3. *Imagine where you might try on some of the behaviors in a safe situation.* After you have selected appropriate skills for your own situation, decide how you might "try on the behaviors." When people are exposed to the skills taught in this book, they often want to try them out in some of the most difficult interpersonal problems at work. They may try effective listening skills at a meeting that is most likely to trigger them into pronouncing judgments. They tend to be assertive with the persons least likely to respond to an assertive message.

   Just as it would be foolhardy to enter a marathon without first trying to jog, it is unwise to use skills in difficult situations before you have tried them in less challenging settings.

4. *Commit yourself to trying a specific skill each week.* The decision to try a specific skill each week is an important commitment. Unless you pin yourself down to a specific skill each week, it is easy to think you are utilizing the skills in this book more than you are. Remember, communication competence is not just knowing a skill, it is also trying a skill.

5. *Reflect on your communication behavior.* Learn to apply "retrospective sense-making" to your own communication acts. Pay attention to how satisfying your communication behavior is to yourself and to your co-workers. After an encounter, learn to ask people such questions as "Well, how do you think that went?" Interpret performance evaluations as statements about your communication. Continue to identify your communication strengths and areas for improvement. Learn to be open to learning and to seeing communication improvement as a "way to be."

# ◆ PART TWO

## SOCIAL ORGANIZATION AND COMMUNICATION

One of the most distinctive features of organizational communication is the concept of social organization. In fact, Gerald Goldhaber defines an organization as *social networks* of interdependent relationships. Members of an organization are interdependent; they affect and are affected by each other. Through everyday contact among people in an organization, individuals in *groups* tend to work, interact, and communicate together.

Social networks and groups give structure and stability to an organization. The formal patterns of networks and the flow of information are often determined by official positions and roles. Since people work together in different groups for different functions, different kinds of groups exist in an organization. A given individual simultaneously may be a member of several groups. In addition, individual employees—isolates—often leave the formal structures or create informal communication linkages and structures.

---

*Organizational networks differ in terms of the*
*quality of their tasks and relationships.*

---

The purpose of this part of the book is to introduce you to organizational networks and the nature of *working relationships*. First, we look at some aspects of the overall group structure of organizations. Second, we discuss some aspects of individual groups, such as functional roles. Finally, we conclude with the interpersonal level of working relationships.

##  THE MACRONETWORKS OF ORGANIZATION

A macronetwork is a repetitive pattern of information transmission among groups in an organization. Perhaps the most commonly understood network is the formal organizational chart. Organizational charts are made up of *positional* relationships defined by the authority, structure, and functional duties of organizational members.

The rationale for creating an organization based on positional relationship was supplied by Max Weber's bureaucratic theory of organizations, discussed in Part One. Many theories of organization agree with the emphasis on positions and list two main advantages:

- Organizing around positions, rather than people, gets tasks accomplished more efficiently.

- Organizing around positions reduces the amount of conflict resulting from different employees doing the same thing.

From a communication perspective, positional relationships help to clarify the nature of relationships and reduce the amount of jealousy, friction, insecurity, and inefficiency that can result from uncertain and ambiguous working relationships.

The most common positional relationship is the *superior–subordinate relationship*. The communication and working relationship between manager and employee is probably the most crucial dynamic to efficient and effective organizational functioning. Subordinates tend to tell superiors what they think the superior wants to hear, what the subordinate wants the superior to hear, and to share information that reflects favorably on the subordinate. The quality of this information can have consequences for the entire organizational structure and performance.

In addition to organizational charts and positions, several types of networks may be overlaid upon an organization, each providing a major function for the organization. But any network consists of two fundamental parts: the members and their links.

*Links* are characterized by five properties:

- *Symmetry*—the degree to which the members connected by a link interact on an equity basis.

- *Strength*—the frequency of interaction among group members.

- *Reciprocity*—the extent to which members agree about their links.

- *Content*—the informational focus of the interaction.

- *Mode*—the channel or means of communicating.

Thus, macronetworks consist of members linked together in various ways to share information. If the members give and take information relatively equally, the link is symmetrical. If the members communicate often, it is strong. If two people believe that they communicate often with one another, the link is reciprocal. The content of the link can be about work, social matters, or some other subject. The information can be communicated face-to-face, through meetings, or by telephone or computer.

The network concept provides a sensible way of looking at organizational structure and function in terms of communication. We now move to the question of the internal structure of groups themselves.

# ◆ THE MICRONETWORKS OF ORGANIZATIONS

Groups themselves tend to have internal structures. A *micronetwork* is the pattern of interaction of a group. Communicating—listening, making statements, asking questions, providing summaries, leading discussions—is how you participate in groups.

Harold Leavitt has identified five different micronetworks (see Figure A). Leavitt found that the central person in a network (e.g., the wheel) usually becomes the leader and enjoys the position more than those on the periphery whose communication is

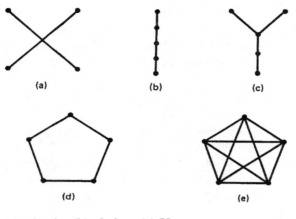

(a) wheel    (b) chain    (c) Y
(d) circle    (e) all-channel

**FIGURE A    MICRONETWORKS**

---

much more restricted. The central person of a group can communicate with any other person, but those on the periphery must direct all their comments through the center. While the chain and the Y networks have the same characteristics as the wheel, the circle and all channel patterns are much less centralized and are sometimes leaderless.

---

*A person who dominates the communication will*
*sometimes create a network similar to the wheel.*

---

Because networks, like the wheel, are centralized, they can result in a dependency on a leader and lower group satisfaction. Likewise, the chain or Y network allows members to communicate with one or two other people, but not with all others in the group. This produces subgroups, decreases satisfaction, and allows a relatively poor amount of information exchange.

---

*The all-channel micronetwork may be relatively slow,*
*but it is superior in terms of information*
*exchange, member satisfaction, and feedback.*

---

Another way of looking at micronetworks is by classifying their *functional roles*. The functional roles of groups can be divided into command (task) and relational (process) roles. This approach is most useful for learning to identify roles and to measure the communication contribution of each role.

Functional group roles are directed toward both accomplishing the group's objective through systematic problem-solving (task) and helping the interpersonal functioning of the group (process). But let's first take a look at some examples of dysfunctional group roles:

- *Placators*—for one reason or another, these people isolate themselves from other group members and turn over decisions to those members. Placators treat the communication system as closed to them by withholding input and denying their own point of view. They may be less secure in their self-concepts or less motivated to accomplish tasks. They can also serve as friendly followers and go along passively.

- *Pouncers*—like to dominate a discussion or decision and tell other group members what they should be doing, how to do it, and who should do it. They tend to intimidate other group members, especially placators, into submission. They like to aggressively give orders and attempt to force others to agree with them. They can also deflate and antagonize others.

- *Distractors*—find a variety of ways to keep the group off the subject or task. They may "nitpick" by dwelling on unimportant issues and nonessential considerations, such as the meaning of words, or use the group to get personal attention or sympathy. While having different motives, distractors direct groups away from goals and toward individual concerns.

- *Computers*—show no interest in the process or human relations aspect of group work. They are extremely task-oriented. They may not want to dominate the group and show no inclination to force opinions, but they desire to finish the task even at the expense of other people's input, feelings, and social interaction. They can also lead a group to make decisions not shared by all members and guarantee poor performance.

Some examples of functional group roles are:

- *Gatekeepers*—praise, agree with, and accept the ideas of others in the group. They encourage the participation of others, especially placators.

- *Harmonizers*—mediate intragroup conflicts and relieve tension, often through appropriate humor. They attempt to create a safe environment for people to participate and contribute. They attempt especially to "harmonize" pouncers.

- *Standard Setters*—raise questions of goals and purpose, express standards for the group, and assess movement toward goals. They are an effective counter to the distractor.

- *Humanizers*—show an interest in the process or human relations aspect of group work. They are process-oriented and offer some balance to "computers." They encourage some discussion of feelings.

Considering the complex dynamic of network characteristics, patterns, and roles, group communication is often said to be synonymous with *exchange*. Group members exchange information, persuasions, and responsibilities for the outcomes of decision-making or problem-solving. The principle of exchange is built on the "give a little, get a little" idea of human relationships. "Giving" contributes to our sense of self-esteem (relational) and participation in the activities around us. "Getting" is our *reward* for making those contributions.

The principle of exchange applies to organizational communication because it can be a way of evaluating participation in groups. At each separate level in an organizational hierarchy, information (or goods, services, and sentiments) is generated between and among people who are responsible for carrying out tasks and maintaining solid working relationships with others. The information produced at one level is consumed at another level as the organization directs the *flow of messages* over a period of time. These exchanges reveal the degree of interdependence between and among organizational groups.

Communication is the articulation of exchanges and reveals that the exchanges are being made. The goals of one person or group usually require the cooperation of other people or groups to be attained. The exchange between and among people has given rise to a theory of participation in working relationships based on the idea of fairness, justice, or the maintenance of equity in the way people respond to each other.

---

*We communicate with others to reach goals.*

---

*Equity theory* summarizes participation in groups with four propositions:

- Group members will try to maximize their goals.
- Groups can maximize collective rewards by developing a system for equitably apportioning resources among members.
- When group members find themselves participating in inequitable relationships, they will experience frustration.
- Group members who experience inequity and frustration will attempt to eliminate the inequity and frustration.

We have outlined some key concepts related to the micronetwork level of organizational communication. We conclude with the interpersonal level of working relationships.

# ◆ INTERPERSONAL WORKING RELATIONSHIPS

Roger Fisher and William Ury, in their book, *Getting to Yes: Negotiating Agreement Without Giving In,* recognize that to have a working relationship, co-workers have to communicate. The quality of a working relationship is measured by the quality of communication. This generalization can be particularly applied to the major kind of organizational relationships—interpersonal.

The most intimate relationship we have with other people at work is interpersonal. In Chapter 3, we offered a definition of interpersonal communication as a quality of communication that emphasizes the uniqueness, choices, and feelings of another person. At this point, we'd like to emphasize another theoretical aspect of interpersonal relationships that applies more directly to the chapters in this part of the book.

In authentic interpersonal relationships, no one is excluded. There is a sense of mutual sharing where members of the relationship define and assert their own identity and interests, pass information with the understanding that they will also receive information, and generally participate in social interaction.

As you'll read in Chapter 5, equity theory can also be used to describe this process of working relationships. *Mutual Reward Theory* (MRT) says that if an individual in a working relationship perceives a discrepancy or "imbalance" in the amount and quality of the information he or she receives and the amount and quality he or she gives, the individual is less motivated to maintain the relationship.

---

*The imbalance or inequity of a working relationship refers to the perceived difference that exists between the communication of two or more people. The difference may be based on command (information) or relational issues.*

---

MRT provides at least one major communication guideline for managers and employees to consider: When individuals believe they are not being rewarded with equitable communication, certain morale and productivity problems may arise.

Interpersonal relationships can exert a powerful and pervasive influence over organizational affairs. Organizational communication theorists Wayne Pace and Don Faules suggest that where equitable conditions for good interpersonal relationships exist, we also tend to find positive responses to supervisors, responsiveness to personal and organizational needs, sensitivity to employee feelings, and a willingness to share information.

# ◆ THE PURPOSE OF PART TWO OF THE BOOK

The purpose of the chapters in Part Two of this book is *to help you see how equitable working relationships make for effective upward and downward communication (vertical) and horizontal communication.*

Chapter 5 will discuss the nature of working relationships, enhancing the discussion of how mutual reward theory describes a satisfactory balance of rewards between people. Chapter 6 will extend these ideas by detailing effective vertical and horizontal working relationships.

Chapter 7 emphasizes that the most important working relationship you must deal with is the one between you and your immediate supervisor. Chapter 8 concludes Part Two with a discussion regarding communication as a team member and how a highly respected team member accepts and promotes certain human relations and communication skills.

# ◆ CHAPTER 5

## UNDERSTANDING THE NATURE OF RELATIONSHIPS

The purpose of this chapter is to look more deeply into the nature of working relationships. To do this we will explore six different characteristics that are often involved. These characteristics can have a considerable influence on the quality or tone of the relationship. In a sense, they constitute the ingredients, or components, of the relationship itself. From another point of view, they represent six human-relations competencies you may wish to possess.

Perhaps you will understand the idea of a relationship better if you visualize it as a biological connection between two fellow employees. Disregard the personalities involved and concentrate on the relationship itself. The following illustrations may help you do this.

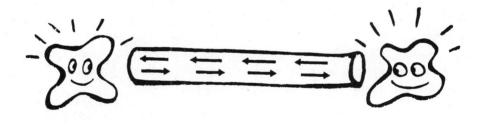

The two-way arrows between the above "bloodcells" remind us that verbal communication is the lifeblood of the relationship. Good input and good reception are necessary at both ends. The following illustration adds to the relationship of those factors we will deal with in this chapter.

Of course, not all of the elements in this illustration are likely to be present in any single relationship. Some relationships may have only one or two. Others may have four or five. An investigation into each of them, however, will give you additional insight into the nature of all working relationships.

## ◆ MUTUAL REWARD THEORY

With proper care, you can create working relationships that will turn out to be mutually rewarding. The *mutual reward theory (MRT)* states that a relationship between two people is enhanced when there is a satisfactory balance of rewards between them. In a good MRT relationship, both parties come out ahead. In fact, if a working relationship is to remain healthy over a long time, it must contribute something of value to both persons. When one individual suddenly discovers that she or he has been contributing substantially more than she or he has been receiving, the relationship can quickly weaken. However, when there is a balanced reward system between people, the working relationship can thrive. The cases of Gabriella and Molly illustrate this theory.

> Gabriella was a quiet, timid, serious worker with outstanding job knowledge. Joseph, on the other hand, was a very outgoing person with great personal confidence but less job knowledge. They worked next to each other in identical jobs and, despite their differences, they slowly built a strong relationship.
>
> How did it happen? Gabriella made a patient effort to teach Joseph as much as possible about the job and took care of some mistakes he made without the supervisor's finding out about them. What did Joseph do in return? He helped Gabriella develop more self-confidence and become a more outgoing person. He did this by paying her deserved compliments, introducing her to co-workers from other departments, and generally giving her a feeling of acceptance that she had not been able to develop by herself.

Because each party contributed to the success of the other (both eventually became supervisors), their relationship became strong and permanent.

Molly worked for Ms. Gonzales for three years before taking over her job as department manager. During that period, MRT was constantly in effect. Molly provided high productivity, loyalty, and dependability to the department and to Ms. Gonzales. Ms. Gonzales, as the supervisor, provided a good learning environment for Molly and gave her the recognition she needed. For example, Ms. Gonzales often introduced Molly to upper-management people and related the progress she was making. This exposure eventually gave Molly the edge she needed to achieve a promotion.

The term *bonding* is currently in popular use to signify a close, emotionally important relationship. In this context, bonding can take place between two co-workers, between an employee and an immediate supervisor, and especially between an employee and a mentor. A working relationship that involves bonding needs to have two characteristics. First, it is important that the relationship not become overly personal to the point where the present productivity and future career of either individual are placed in jeopardy. Second, it is vital to the longevity of the relationship that it be mutually rewarding so that both parties benefit somewhat equally.

Relationships can be mutually rewarding because people can strengthen each other in many different ways. Obviously, however, when one person does all the giving, deterioration quickly sets in. As you build new relationships and protect old ones, look for things you can do to contribute to the success and happiness of the person next to you. When you do this, you will almost always receive something in return that will make life better for you. If you weave MRT into your behavior, you demonstrate a significant human-relations competency.

## ◆ VALUE CONFLICTS

Everyone has his or her own value system. Everyone has his or her own priority list of what is really important in life. Different people seek different lifestyles. Because of this, it is only natural that value conflicts exist between people who are forced to associate with each other closely in the world of work. Here are two typical examples.

Tony was assigned to work next to Mr. Henderson, who was more than twice his age. Tony was a bachelor who enjoyed an active social life and did not want to assume family responsibilities too soon. He was determined to have a lifestyle different from that of his parents. His foreign sports car and fashionable clothing reflected this attitude. Mr. Henderson, on the other hand, was a family-oriented, religious person.

How did they learn to work together gracefully? At the beginning, they both played it cool and built their relationship exclusively on the basis of job factors. Tony learned to respect Mr. Henderson for his many years of job experience and his willingness to share it. Mr. Henderson learned to respect Tony for his willingness to learn and contribute a full day's work. After six months they could even discuss their value differences. A better mutual understanding was brought about.

Beverly was brought up in a strict home environment and was taught to respect discipline. She was considered fairly square by her contemporaries. Trish, on the other hand, was very happy-go-lucky and undisciplined. She considered herself very much ahead of others of her generation. How did Beverly and Trish get along when they were forced to work very closely together? At first, the sparks of conflict were rather obvious. But slowly they built a sound working relationship based upon their mutual desire to do a good job for the company and further their careers. They did not become close personal friends, and they did not go out together socially. However, they learned to respect each other, and both benefited from the working relationship despite their value differences.

It is a mistake, perhaps even an invasion of privacy, to impose one's own values on another, especially in the work environment. What a fellow worker does with her private life is her own business and should have nothing to do with the relationship you build with her on the job. To react to an individual in a negative way for what she does on the outside should be avoided. Common interests on the job should provide a sufficient basis for a good working relationship. You will be surprised how many good working relationships you can build with people who think and live differently than you do.

◆ **ETHNIC IMPLICATIONS**

Years ago white males were dominant in numbers and positions of authority in most organizations. Today there is more diversity at all levels. Some firms employ more women than men, with increasing numbers in executive roles; others employ a high percentage from Asian and other cultures. Depending upon the mix within your organization, you can react in three different ways:

1. If you are in the dominant culture, you can maintain a negative attitude toward those in others. Those who do this rarely learn to work with others successfully, and their careers suffer.

2. If you are in a minority culture, you can try so hard to be one of "them" that you lose your own identity at great expense to your own positive attitude and job productivity.

3. Regardless of the position you occupy, if you adapt to all cultures in your organization you will become a better person to know, you will be more productive, and your career will be enhanced.

A major attitude change is taking place in the United States. When our country was young, many people thought that we would become one culture with a single language and concentrate 100 percent on our own traditions. It didn't happen that way. Today, instead of being a great "melting pot," we are more like a "great mosaic" created out of different cultures.

Accepting this "international" or "mosaic" view may assist you in building strong and lasting relationships with the many different people you will meet in your workplace. It will also help you maintain your positive attitude.

A basic competency is to respect and treat each person as a unique and special individual. Look beyond outward appearances, ignore how he or she might resemble someone you had an unfavorable experience with in the past, and accept each person as a unique individual. If everyone could sincerely adhere to this one fundamental practice, relationships would have a good chance of functioning harmoniously. Each person—and each relationship—would stand on its own, without reference to ethnic background. Unfortunately for all of us, not enough people practice this principle. Here are two short cases to illustrate the point.

Although she had always believed she was free of prejudice, Jean had very little close contact with blacks. She was therefore a little uneasy about working closely with a black person for the first time. Hobart, a young black, joined the department and, after introductions, Jean's uneasiness gave way to anticipation. Hobart was a very easygoing, friendly guy. He would be fun to work with.

Everything went well as far as their relationship was concerned until Hobart started to make a number of mistakes. He kept asking what Jean felt were stupid questions and, in general, he did not live up to her expectations. Jean became so frustrated over the matter that she was tempted to go to her supervisor.

Then, all of a sudden, it came to her that she was expecting more of Hobart because he was black. She was looking for things to complain about instead of being understanding, as she would normally be with a white person. Jean decided to get the relationship back on a fair footing, so she invited Hobart for coffee and admitted her mistake. It was a good move because Hobart had felt Jean's negative attitude and wanted to build a better relationship himself.

Fernando and Archie were assigned two months ago to work as a team on a moving van. Archie had graduated from a community college and hoped eventually to get into management. Fernando was a high school graduate with more than three years' experience in the furniture-moving business.

Archie learned quickly that Fernando was an outstanding worker with excellent skills. He also learned in a hurry that Fernando was not much of a talker. In fact, Fernando communicated only when it was necessary to get the job done.

This silence soon got on Archie's nerves. After making many attempts to get a light conversation going, he decided that Fernando had a lot of deep-seated hostility toward Anglos. It was a very uncomfortable situation and, because Archie needed to talk, he soon became a little bitter about the situation. Should he ask for a transfer? Should he resign?

Then one day it occurred to him that, with a few beers, Fernando might open up and they could learn to communicate. He invited Fernando to be his guest, and they went to a place close to Fernando's home. It was a small place that reflected the Chicano culture. Sure enough, it wasn't long before Fernando felt sufficiently comfortable to start talking.

Archie learned a great deal. Fernando had been pushed around by many people. He did not feel accepted. His silence was more a defense than anything else. But what got to Archie was the fact that Fernando felt that Archie was against *him,* and not the other was around.

It was a revelation for both parties, and much of the tension that had been present on the job was gone the next day. Archie and Fernando had learned how to communicate. As a result, they started to work much better as a team. They didn't become personal friends, but they gained a high degree of mutual respect.

There are many relationships ahead of you that will involve people from different ethnic backgrounds. These relationships will not always be easy to build and maintain. Sometimes they may demand more perception than you possess. Yet, if you are open, honest, sincere, and willing to talk, your chances of building sound MRT relationships are excellent. In doing this, it is good to keep in mind that discussions of religious, political, and cultural differences do not belong in the workplace. If you judge others in ways they do not wish to be judged, they may do the same to you.

## ◆ SEXUAL OVERTONES AND HARASSMENT

Working relationships between employees frequently contain sexual overtones. For the most part, this sexual tension is not dangerous and has little important influence on productivity one way or the other. But not always. Take the case of Judy.

Judy was attracted sexually to her supervisor from the moment he was transferred to her department. A perceptive observer would have noticed that the very next day she started wearing the best clothes in her wardrobe. She became more particular about her makeup. She started working harder to win the favor of her new boss and to create more opportunities to talk with him on business matters.

So what happened? The other women in Judy's department quickly sensed the sexual overtones to the relationship, and their positive attitude toward Judy began to cool. They became more distant, less willing to help her, and less tolerant of her mistakes. It didn't take long for a certain strain to develop among all the employees in the department, and productivity began to suffer.

Judy's case raises a very difficult question: *What are the human relations dangers involved in dating someone where you work?*

There is little danger involved, provided that the individual is not your supervisor, he or she works in a section separated from yours, and you are smart enough to keep your business and personal worlds separate. Under these circumstances, management will probably be very understanding.

There are some real dangers that you should know about in advance, however. Most of them occur under the following circumstances: 1) when a supervisor dates someone in his or her own department, immediate cries of favoritism are raised and productivity is hurt; 2) when two people—especially if they are in the same section—date and do not keep their business and personal worlds separate, relationships with others are hurt and eventually productivity is lowered; and 3) when one or both parties are married, a sticky situation is created that can produce harmful gossip, hurt productivity, and sometimes make it necessary for management to step in.

Before you create or accept a dating situation where you work, you should also consider the chance of a breakup between the two of you later. This could hurt both people involved and leave bad feelings among fellow employees who were in on the matter and took sides.

*Sexual harassment involves something beyond natural overtones.* Sexual harassment in the workplace is behavior of a sexual nature that causes a co-worker to be uncomfortable and has a negative impact on productivity. In most cases, sexual harassment is not one isolated incident. Rather, it is behavior pursued in a deliberate way over a period of time.

There are three forms of harassment: 1) *verbal:* examples are telling risqué jokes, commenting on one's sexual anatomy, pursuing an unwanted relationship, and asking for sexual favors; 2) *visual:* examples are wearing suggestive attire, staring at someone's anatomy, flirting nonverbally, and sitting in a revealing position; 3) *physical:* examples are touching, standing too close, giving a "too lengthy" handshake, and excessive hugging.

Sexual harassment violates the law and inhibits work performance. Victims can be male or female, a manager or subordinate, a vendor or customer. When an individual believes she or he is being sexually harassed, the following steps are recommended: 1) take your complaint to your immediate supervisor; 2) provide the specifics and dates involved; 3) document any further harassment while waiting for the supervisor to correct the situation; 4) if further action is necessary, file a formal complaint with the director of human resources or a superior other than your immediate supervisor; 5) if the source of the harassment happens to be your supervisor, the first step should be to speak to his or her superior.

## ◆ AGE DIFFERENCES

The new employee who is young, capable, and ambitious is faced with a peculiar challenge in most organizations—and it doesn't take long for the challenge to occur. You hear it expressed in many ways:

"I could have had that last promotion if I had had more seniority."

"Everyone in this outfit has age, seniority, or experience beyond mine. I'll never get a chance. I'm wasting my time and ability. I won't get a chance to show what I can do until I'm thirty."

"I think I'll grow a mustache, so that I'll at least appear older."

Many employees between the ages of eighteen and thirty consider their youth a handicap. Some feel that they must put in time to reach a certain age level before they will be given a chance to demonstrate their ability. In a few cases, the situation becomes aggravated because the employee appears younger than he or she actually is.

It is easy to appreciate this attitude if you put yourself in the place of a young employee. He or she sees older, more experienced employees everywhere and may begin to feel that the generation gap is wider inside a business organization than outside, yet he or she wants to make progress, wants to move, and doesn't want to wait. So the pressure builds.

Yet, it is not unusual today to find young supervisors in charge of employees many years their senior. Apparently some young people have the human-relations skills to compensate for their youth. Take the cases of Laurel and Leonard as examples.

Laurel manages a large fashion department in a major department store. The department had sales of over $1 million last year. Laurel supervises nine full-time people, all of whom are at least twice her age, which is twenty. The problems are constant and the pressure is great, but, without exception, the older workers consider her an excellent manager, and her boss feels she has a great future.

Leonard, who is just twenty-three and has only one year of college behind him, is the manager of a large, popular restaurant. Two of the three managers who work under him are much older than he, and one is old enough to be his father. In fact, most of the regular employees are older than he. The establishment is open twenty-four hours a day, and the problems never end. Yet

Leonard seems to be on top of everything, and the president of the chain feels that he is just getting started.

How do young people like Laurel and Leonard do it?

They demonstrate early that they can accept and handle responsibility. They demonstrate that they can make mature decisions. They demonstrate great personal confidence. But, most of all, they demonstrate skills in human relations. They show that they can build strong MRT relationships with older and more experienced employees and management personnel, as well as with people their own age. The fact is that your more mature fellow workers will not resist your progress if you go about it in the right way. Rather, they will want you to succeed and will be willing to help you.

Your decision, then, is a simple one. If you are ambitious, you can either drift along until you are older and have more experience, or you can face the human-relations challenge now and speed up your progress. If you decide to make the effort, there are, among others, two important rewards you should provide in building a relationship with a more mature, experienced person.

*Everyone, regardless of age, likes to be noticed.* This is especially true of older employees. They like to receive compliments (even if the compliments border on flattery). They like to feel that they are still important as employees and as people. They need to feel appreciated and respected. They like to receive credit when due.

The more mature person often likes to keep a young image. Any action that tends to make a mature person feel out of touch or out of date is a mistake. Try to make him or her feel that he still has a lot to offer, that he is part of today's world, not yesterday's. Make a big effort to keep the communication lines open at all times. Do not isolate yourself from this person. Seek his advice. Always include him in your plans for any job-related social activities. Remember, you cannot expect a good vertical relationship with him—should you become his supervisor later on—unless you build a good horizontal working relationship with him now.

Perhaps the most important aspect of building good relationships with mature employees is learning how to gain their respect. This is usually done through ability, hard work, and reliability on a day-to-day basis. Deeds will do more than words. Statistics will do more than promises. Performance will do more than flattery.

More than anything else, learn from this person. Her additional years of experience have taught her many things that you can learn without having to experience them. You can learn through osmosis. Then, if the time comes for you to move ahead, give her credit for making it possible. Let her have the satisfaction of calling you her protégé. Let her take pride in your success.

It will be wise of you to keep your relationship on a formal basis until she gives you the signal to be more relaxed and personal.

What about reversing the situation? How can the mature worker build better relationships with the new, younger employee? There are many steps that can be taken. Here are three that will be greatly appreciated: 1) be patient with new employees' adjustment problems, 2) help them learn by sharing your experience with them, and 3) if needed, give them the confidence to communicate with you.

## ◆ IRRITATION THRESHOLD

Relationships are frequently endangered because one of the individuals has an irritating habit or mannerism that bothers the other. Here are some common ones:

- Harsh or loud voice
- Irritating laugh
- Overbearing manner
- Constant name dropping
- Constant talk about money
- Constant reference to sex
- Telling dirty or unfunny stories
- Overuse of certain words or expressions
- Constant discussion of personal problems
- Constant complaining
- Constant bragging about their successes off the job or the successes of their children

Whether or not a habit or mannerism becomes an irritant depends upon the threshold or *tolerance level* of the second party. If one party has a high enough threshold, he or she may not even notice something that might bother someone else. On the other hand, it is possible for an individual to have a very low threshold for a certain mannerism, in which case the habit can do considerable damage to the relationship.

Diane is an excellent example of a young employee who hurt her relationship with a few fellow workers because of a nervous giggle that followed almost every sentence she uttered. Unfortunately, Diane had no idea what was happening. She was not conscious of the habit or of the fact that it was hurting her relationships with certain people who had low irritation thresholds. One day, after getting a complaint from a good employee who worked next to Diane, the supervisor had a talk with her about it and, thanks to some very hard work on Diane's part, the irritating mannerism all but disappeared in a few weeks.

Once the individual knows about them, bad habits can usually be modified and sometimes eliminated. But the person at the other end of the relationship must not expect too much too soon. In some cases it may be necessary to learn to live with certain irritants by making an attempt to raise one's tolerance level. Seldom do such irritants come from only one side of the relationship. Almost all of us have at least a few mannerisms or habits that bother other people. The individual, even in the business environment, retains the right to remain pretty much the way he or she is, so some adjustment on your part to such factors will be necessary in most relationships. Tolerance, obviously, is a human-relations skill that must be developed.

# ◆ CHAPTER 6
## VERTICAL AND HORIZONTAL WORKING RELATIONSHIPS

Understanding yourself and the power of your positive attitude makes it much easier to meet new people and establish meaningful relationships with them. For example, when you meet a supervisor or co-worker for the first time, a psychological reaction takes place: each person instantaneously interprets the other. It is a feeling that is hard to define. You know something is happening, but you can't put your finger on it. Slowly, as you and the other individual see each other more frequently and get to know each other better, these initial feelings mature into what is called a *relationship*.

A relationship is a *feeling thing* that exists between two people who associate with each other. You can't see, taste, smell, or touch a relationship; you can only feel it in a psychological sense. Job relationships are usually different from social relationships. Job relationships exist only because you selected a certain company and were assigned to work with certain people in a specific department. In other words, in your social life you have a choice; on the job, you do not. Nevertheless, working relationships are extremely important to you and your future because they will have a strong influence on your personality and personal productivity.

Working relationships of this nature are fascinating to study. For example, one interesting characteristic is that two persons cannot meet regularly on the job or work in the same general areas *without* having a relationship. So the first thing to learn about working relationships is that, whether you like it or not, one will exist between you and every employee or supervisor with whom you have regular contact.

- You need not work next to this person.

- You need not speak to this person.

- You need not even have a desire to know this person.

Yet, a relationship will exist. There appears to be no way to neutralize a relationship under these conditions. The very fact that you might decide to ignore a person does not destroy the relationship; in fact, the opposite may happen—the relationship may become more tense and psychologically powerful. Let us take a specific example.

You notice an employee working in a department next to you. In an attempt to be friendly, you say hello in a very pleasant way to this person the first day on the job, and you receive no reply.

Does this mean that the relationship is cut off at this point?

Far from it! You may feel that her failure to reply is a slight to you, and this may naturally disturb you. You may decide not to take the initiative again. Nevertheless, you will remember this person clearly and wonder what will happen in the future.

The person to whom you said hello, on the other hand, has had some kind of reaction to your friendly gesture. She may feel that she treated you in an unfriendly manner (perhaps she was not feeling well that day) and might welcome another opportunity to be more friendly. Or, she may have interpreted your hello as being a little too forward on your part as a new employee and decided to be cool toward you.

You could ignore her. You could avoid verbal contact. You and she could see each other only a few times a week.

Would a relationship exist?

Yes, indeed. Two persons have made contact with each other. They see each other occasionally. They work for the same company. As long as these factors exist, a relationship must exist. Under these conditions you cannot erase a relationship. The attempt on the part of one person to withdraw serves only to make the relationship more emotionally charged; it does not in any manner eliminate it.

---

*You cannot consistently work with or near people*
*or communicate with them frequently without*
*having working relationships with them.*

---

There is another interesting characteristic about these relationships when viewed objectively. They are either strong or weak, warm or cool, healthy or unhealthy, friendly or distant. There appears to be no absolute neutral ground. Every relationship has a very small positive or negative content.

Have you ever heard someone say, "I can take her or leave her"? The phrase usually means that it doesn't make any difference whether the person referred to is around or not. But the very fact that one makes such a comment indicates that it would be better if the person were not around. The relationship still exists, and in this case it is a little cool.

A third characteristic is that each relationship is different. You must build relationships with all kinds of people, regardless of race, religion, age, sex, or personality characteristics. Each relationship will be unique. Each will be built on a different basis. Each will have its own integrity.

As you look around and study your co-workers and your supervisor, you will see that they are all separate personalities. At the same time, your supervisor and co-workers are studying you. Do they all see the same person?

Strange as it may seem, they do not. You do not look the same to different people. You make a different impression on each of them because they interpret you differently.

There is another way of saying this: you do not have a single personality in the eyes of others. Each person interprets you differently, based on his or her own unique background, prejudices, likes, dislikes, and so on. Your personality, to that person, is different. The way he or she interprets your personality *is* your personality to that person.

Why all this emphasis on the way in which people view your personality? How will this help you become more sensitive to human relationships?

Here is your answer: Because everybody sees you differently, you will have to build good relationships with different people differently. And make no mistake here, *good relationships must be built.* They seldom come about automatically.

You will rarely build a strong, warm, or healthy relationship with two persons in the same way. You will always have to take into consideration the person at the other end of the relationship.

Some people are not going to interpret your personality favorably to start with. You are going to have to be sensitive enough to determine who these people are, and then you must build a good relationship with them on an individual basis. It is not easy to change a cool relationship to a warm one, yet you cannot afford to allow it to remain in an unhealthy state. You should make some effort to build it into a stronger relationship. To do this, you should consider the person at the other end of the relationship and remember that he or she sees you differently than anyone else does.

Now that you have a good picture of just what is meant by a relationship, it is time to talk about the two kinds of relationships.

First, we will discuss the *vertical working relationship.* This is the relationship between you and your immediate supervisor. If, as a regular employee, you have two or more supervisors, you will have two or more vertical relationships to maintain. Normally, you will have one immediate supervisor, as illustrated.

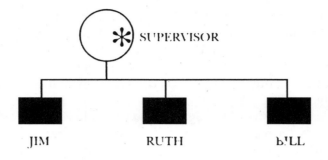

In a small department consisting of one supervisor and three employees, each employee has a different vertical relationship with the same supervisor. This relationship is indicated by the line between each employee and the supervisor. This is often called the *job-relations line.* If the relationship is strong, we indicate this by a heavy line. If it is weak, we indicate this by a light line. Naturally, it is almost impossible for supervisors to create and maintain an equally strong line between themselves and all the employees in the department. It is their job to try to do this, and the closer they come to this ideal, the better it is for the department. But supervisors are human beings and are not perfect. Consequently, the job-relations lines are seldom equally strong. The person working next to you might have either a stronger or a weaker relationship with the supervisor than you have.

You will notice in the following illustration that arrows have been added to the lines.

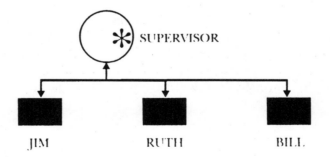

These arrows at the ends of the vertical job-relations lines have real significance. They signify that there should be a free flow of information between the workers and the supervisor. It is extremely difficult for a strong relationship to exist between two persons without two-way communication. The supervisor must feel free to discuss, openly and frankly, certain problems with Ruth, Jim, and Bill. If the supervisor hesitates to talk with Jim about a certain weakness in his job performance, the relationship between the two of them is not what it could be. By the same token, if Jim is hesitant about taking a suggestion or a gripe to the supervisor, the relationship is less than ideal.

*The lifeblood of a good relationship
is free and open communication.*

Good relationships are built and maintained by free and frequent verbal communication. People need to talk with each other, exchange ideas, voice complaints, and offer suggestions if they intend to keep a good relationship. The moment that one party refuses to talk things over, the relationship line becomes thin and weak.

The primary responsibility for creating and maintaining a strong vertical relationship rests with the supervisor. This is a responsibility that goes with the position. If the relationship line is in need of repair, it is primarily the supervisor's responsibility to initiate a discussion that can mend the break.

Although the supervisor has the primary responsibility, you as the employee have the secondary responsibility to keep the relationship line strong and healthy. Some employees make the serious mistake of thinking that the supervisor is wholly responsible for making them happy and productive.

Chapter 7 will show you how to create and maintain a good relationship with your supervisor. It suffices now to say that you can't expect the supervisor to do all the relationship building. You will have to work hard to keep a good job-relations line between you and your supervisor. Even if you have an exceptionally poor supervisor, you will have to meet him or her halfway. Vertical relationships need to be in healthy repair if departmental productivity is to be high. Often the supervisor finds that it requires a great deal of tact and delicacy to maintain vertical relationships—small wonder that management has seen fit to give this person some special training.

*The horizontal working relationship is also important to you.*

Horizontal working relationships are those that exist between you and fellow workers in the same department—the people you work next to on an hour-to-hour, day-to-day basis. The following diagram illustrates the horizontal relationships among three people in a very small department.

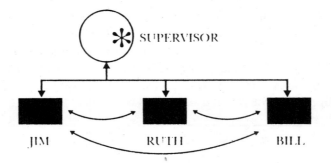

You will note that Jim has a horizontal working relationship with both Ruth and Bill. In this very small department of three employees and one supervisor, Jim has one vertical relationship and two horizontal relationships to keep strong. It is easy to see that in larger departments there would be many more. In fact, the average number of employees in a department is nine.

You (not the supervisor) have the primary responsibility for creating and keeping healthy horizontal relationships. The supervisor—working at a distance in regard to these relationships—has the secondary responsibility. Once in a while he or she might find it necessary to step in to help restore a good relationship between two employees. But, by and large, the supervisor must leave this up to the employees themselves.

The critical need for building good horizontal working relationships is often ignored by some workers. When they permit this to happen, their doors of opportunity are locked and the keys are thrown away.

*It is extremely important to the new employee to build and maintain good horizontal working relationships.* In fact, this should be a major part of your total human-relations effort as you start your career. Much of this book is devoted to the principles and techniques that will assist you in this respect. For example, here are two mistakes you should refrain from making.

1. Avoid concentrating on building a good relationship with your supervisor and neglecting good relationships with your fellow workers.

2. Avoid concentrating on building one or two very strong horizontal working relationships and neglecting those with the remaining fellow workers in your department.

Making either mistake will cause immediate disharmony in your department and will put you in human-relations hot water. The supervisor cannot afford to have an extremely strong relationship with you and weak relationships with your fellow workers if he or she wants high productivity from all. It makes for dissension and immediate cries of favoritism.

From your point of view, then, an overly strong vertical relationship can cause a general weakening of your horizontal working relationships. When you make the mistake of concentrating on one or two horizontal working relationships, the remaining horizontal relationships deteriorate and your vertical relationship with the supervisor is also weakened.

*All horizontal working relationships in the same department should be given equal attention and consideration.* One should not be strengthened at the expense of others, even though it may be more fun and more satisfying. Balance is important.

*When you concentrate on creating good horizontal working relationships with all fellow workers, you almost automatically create a good vertical relationship with your supervisor.* It should be recognized, of course, that the success of this principle is assured only if the supervisor is sufficiently sensitive to know what is going on. In the majority of cases, this is a fair assumption. A perceptive supervisor will greatly appreciate any employee who builds a better team spirit in the department by creating and maintaining strong horizontal working relationships.

There are, of course, important relationships other than those indicated in the diagram. Your relationship-building activity should not be confined to a single department. It is a good idea for you to expand your sphere of influence as quickly as possible on your new job. The more good relationships you build, the better.

As important as peripheral relationships are, they are not your primary working relationships. You cannot afford to concentrate on building relationships outside your department by neglecting those on the inside.

The building of a strong vertical relationship with your immediate supervisor and strong horizontal working relationships with your fellow workers is absolutely essential to your personal success. No other human-relations activity should have a higher priority.

# ◆CHAPTER 7

## COMMUNICATING WITH YOUR MANAGER

The most important working relationship you must deal with is the one between you and your immediate supervisor. This single relationship can speed up your personal progress or slow it down to a discouraging crawl. It can make going to work a joy or a drag. It can prepare you for greater responsibilities or it can frustrate your desire to learn. And there is just no way to avoid the human-relations fact that, good or bad, you must learn to cope with your boss.

What kind of person will you draw as a supervisor?

It is impossible to predict. However, he (or she) will be basically the same person he used to be when he held a job similar to yours, except that now he has much more responsibility. He may or may not have been given some special training to help him become a good supervisor. He may be easy to get along with or he may be very difficult. He may be sensitive to your needs or he may be insensitive. He may be feeling his way along and making many mistakes, or he may be highly experienced and a real pro at this job.

Three things are certain about your supervisor, however: 1) he probably has a strong personality that gave him the confidence to become a supervisor in the first place, 2) the responsibilities of being a supervisor probably weigh heavily on his shoulders, and 3) he has work authority over you.

What is a supervisor?

He or she is a *teacher*. He will not only teach you the routine of your new job, but he will also have a great influence on your attitude toward your job and the company. He has a reservoir of knowledge, skills, and techniques that you need to learn. You will be most fortunate if he is a good teacher. If he is not, you will have to learn from observation.

He is a *counselor*. His job is to see that you live up to your potential. He may need to correct errors you are making. He may need to give you tips on improving yourself as an employee. He may feel the need to have a heart-to-heart talk with you at times.

He is a *leader*. More than anything else, your supervisor must provide the leadership your department requires. He must provide motivation for all employees. He must earn your respect—not by being soft and easy, but by being a strong leader who will help you build a long-range career.

It would be a mistake to attempt to type supervisors. They cannot be clearly classified into different groups. Each supervisor has a unique personality. Each has his or her own style.

Do you recall your early school days, when you discovered the differences between teachers? You may have had one who expected a great deal more from you than the others. You may not have liked this person at the time, but years later you came to realize how much this one teacher had taught you. The same can be true with supervisors.

If you are ambitious, you don't want an easygoing supervisor who does not care and, as a result, hinders instead of helps your progress. You will be better off with a more concerned, more demanding supervisor who will help you reach your potential. With an easy supervisor, you might develop some poor working habits and eventually become unhappy with yourself. With a strong supervisor, one who will take time to train you, you will become a better worker and improve your future. But no matter what kind of boss you encounter, it is up to you to learn to understand him and work efficiently under his kind of leadership.

*You* should do some of the adjusting.

*You* should provide some of the understanding.

*You* should help build the relationship that must exist between the two of you.

*You* should communicate effectively.

Each supervisor creates his or her own special communication climate, or atmosphere, under which you must operate. The following analysis of three kinds of climates may give you some indication of the adjustments you might have to make in the future.

## ◆ THE STRUCTURED COMMUNICATION CLIMATE

Some supervisors are more strict than others. They operate a tight department by keeping close, and sometimes restrictive, controls. They frequently expect employees to be precisely on time, orderly, and highly efficient. They permit foolishness only when a special occasion calls for it. Ninety-eight percent of the time they stick strictly to business.

The supervisor who creates this kind of atmosphere often appears cold, distant, and unfeeling to the new employee. He or she seems unreachable. As a result, the new employee may begin to fear this person.

Some jobs force supervisors to be autocratic. Some kinds of work require very high safety standards and efficiency. For example, a producer of a television program might have to be autocratic in order to maintain the split-second efficiency required. Work of a highly technical nature, in which certain precision standards must be met, will call for a different climate than work in a service field.

Although the supervisor who establishes this kind of atmosphere may appear cold and unapproachable, the opposite is often true. He or she is probably more interested in you and more willing to help than you suspect.

## ◆ THE PERMISSIVE COMMUNICATION CLIMATE

The direct opposite of the structured climate is the permissive atmosphere. Some supervisors have a free-and-easy leadership style. There is no apparent intervention, and there are few controls or restrictions.

The permissive climate can be the most dangerous of all, especially for the inexperienced employee, because his or her need for self-discipline is so great. The employee who does not feel the presence of a leader may not make good use of time. The employee may find it difficult to develop self-motivation. If things are too easygoing, he or she may relax too much and become too friendly with fellow workers. All of this can create bad habits that will ultimately lead to mutual dissatisfaction. Instead of being an ideal situation, then, the permissive climate becomes a trap that can destroy the desire to succeed and eventually cause great unhappiness.

Whether we like to accept it or not, a structured climate often gives us more job security and forces us to live closer to our potential. Beware of a climate that is too relaxed unless you are a self-starter and can discipline yourself. You might discover that too much freedom is your downfall.

## ◆ THE DEMOCRATIC COMMUNICATION CLIMATE

The goal of most supervisors in modern organizations is to create a democratic climate. This atmosphere is the most difficult of all to establish. In fact, purely democratic action is often a goal rather than a reality.

A democratic climate is one in which the employees want to do what the supervisor wants done. The supervisor becomes one of the group and still retains his or her leadership role. The employees are permitted to have a great deal to say about the operation of the department. Everyone becomes involved because each person works from inside the group rather than from outside. The supervisor is the leader and a member of the group at the same time. As a result, a team feeling is created. Many isolated cases of research indicate that most people experience greater personal satisfaction and respond with greater productivity if the supervisor can create and maintain a democratic atmosphere.

If this is true, why can't more supervisors achieve this kind of climate? There are many reasons.

In the first place, it is the most difficult climate to create, and once created, the most difficult to maintain. It requires a real expert, an individual with great skill and sensitivity; *one should not expect to find a large number of supervisors with this ability.*

In the second place, not all workers respond to this climate, ideal as it may seem. You may like it best, but others in your department may like a more autocratic approach. This is especially true when there are young workers in a department where many more experienced and older employees work. You will often hear employees say: "I wish he would quit fooling around and tell us what to do" or "I wish she would tighten up things around here—those people are getting away with murder" or "He is too easy. I can't enjoy working for someone who doesn't set things down clearly and specifically from the beginning."

In the third place, the supervisor who aspires to build a true democratic climate always exists somewhere between the structured and the permissive. He or she may approach the ideal situation for a while, only to find that a few employees are taking advantage of the situation. When this happens it is necessary to tighten up again and become more structured.

All supervisors must create and maintain what some people refer to as a *discipline line*. This is an imaginary line or point beyond which the employee senses she or he should not pass lest some form of disapproval and possible disciplinary action take place. It is important to keep a consistent discipline line. Some supervisors claim that keeping a firm but comfortable one is a tightrope they walk each day on the job.

You may hear your supervisor or a college professor discuss Theory X and Theory Y. *Theory X* (representing a more structured climate) supports management by control. It states that the worker should be directed and controlled in order to achieve high productivity. A basic assumption is that most employees are not self-motivated. Leaders with a Theory X orientation often reach consistently high productivity levels in their departments. They also have the reputation of doing an excellent job in training their employees.

*Theory Y* (representing a more democratic/permissive climate) encourages participative management. It states that workers will achieve greater productivity if they can set their own goals and direct their own efforts through involvement. The theory assumes that under the proper working climate, workers will motivate themselves. A discipline line is maintained at a lower level. Theory Y leaders who are sufficiently skillful to achieve high productivity demonstrate a high level of leadership talent that often attracts the attention of upper management.

Every supervisor creates an individual climate. Some supervisors come up with a workable blend of the structured and democratic. Others come up with a blend of the permissive and democratic. We call this their *management,* or *leadership, style.*

Whether we personally like a supervisor or his or her style is not as important as whether we can learn to be productive in the climate this person creates. The new worker should not be too quick to judge, however, because it is often true that what appears to be a difficult climate at the beginning might turn out to be a comfortable and beneficial one later on. So whatever the *style* of the supervisor you draw, it will be your responsibility to build the best possible relationship with him or her. Your career progress may depend upon it. To help you meet this challenge, here are ten tips that should assist you.

1. *Avoid communicating to your supervisor the negative attitudes you may have developed toward other authority figures in your life.* Some people who have had problems with other supervisors, parents, teachers, and similar authority figures make the mistake of transferring their feelings of hostility to their new supervisor. This is unfair. Wipe away any previous negative feelings you may have, and give your new (or present) boss an opportunity to build a healthy relationship with you. If you give her or him a fair chance, she will almost always earn your respect instead of your hostility.

2. *Expect some rough days under her supervision.* Everyone, including supervisors, is entitled to a few bad days. Your boss is only human. If she should boil over on a given day, don't let it throw you. If she seems to be picking on you for a while, give her time to get over it. More important than anything else, try not to take personally anything she does that you don't like. There may be times when you do not understand your boss's behavior, but if you can float along with it, chances are good that it won't last long.

3. *Refuse to nurse a small gripe into a major issue.* A small gripe, when nurtured, can get blown out of proportion and can lead to a confrontation with your supervisor that will hurt your relationship. If you have a legitimate gripe, try to talk it over with her quickly so that you can get it out of your system before it builds up. Remember, she won't know you have a complaint unless you tell her.

4. *Select the right time to approach your supervisor.* Whether you have a complaint or a positive suggestion to make, try to approach your supervisor at the right time. She may be too busy or under too much pressure on a given day to talk to you. If so, wait it out. When the pressure is off, chances are good that she will give you a fair opportunity. However, if you do try to talk to her at a bad time and are turned off, wait until another day and try again. If it is important to you, she will no doubt want to talk to you about it. Give her another chance.

5. *Never go over your supervisor's head without talking to her first.* The easiest and quickest way to destroy your relationship with your supervisor is to go over her head on a problem that involves her or his department.

Always talk to your supervisor first. If you are not satisfied with the results, you can then take other action. At least this way your supervisor will know that you consulted her first.

6. *Try not to let your supervisor intimidate you.* Keep in mind that she may not be a professional. She could be guilty of playing favorites or other forms of nonprofessional behavior. Such behavior could cause you to fear your boss. Fear is a strong emotion. If you become so fearful of your boss that you cannot approach her, you should talk to someone in the human resources department, consider a possible transfer, or, if necessary, resign. You will never be happy working for a person you fear, and a supervisor will seldom respect you if you are afraid of her.

7. *It can be a human-relations mistake to make a buddy of your supervisor.* Your relationship with your supervisor is a business relationship. Keep it that way. The distance between you and your boss may often appear to be a fine line, but she is still your boss. If you get too personal, it will almost always turn out badly.

8. *In case you make a mistake, clear the air quickly.* If you make a serious goof and injure your relationship with your boss, why not clean the slate with an open discussion? It is a good idea to leave work every day with a pleasant feeling toward your job and your supervisor. If you have had trouble with her on a given day and truly believe that it is partly your fault, the mature thing to do is to accept your share of the blame. You will feel better and so will your supervisor.

9. *Remember that not all supervisors enjoy their roles.* A surprising number of supervisors would really prefer to be workers, but they have accepted their promotions because management has pressed them to do so, because they feel they can contribute more as supervisors, or because they can make more money to help their families. As an employee, you should view this as a possibility. It will give you more insight into the role itself and perhaps help you tolerate your supervisor more easily. Try to remember that being a good supervisor is difficult. Sometimes those who try the hardest to win the respect of their workers never fully succeed because of personality traits they cannot change.

10. *When possible, convert your supervisor into a mentor.* A mentor is a person in a key position who takes a personal interest in your career and acts as an adviser. Your present supervisor may be on her way up in your organization. If you build the right relationship with her, she might counsel and guide you over a period of time, even though she may no longer be your supervisor. You might even ride her coattails to the top.

It should be remembered, however, that ethical behavior on the part of both you and your supervisor is essential if the relationship is to be strong and lasting. To maintain your side of the bargain, the following tips are presented.

- Maintain open and honest communication. Tell the whole story regarding any problems that develop. The moment deception appears, the relationship is permanently injured.

- Do not discuss your supervisor in a negative way with co-workers. It communicates an absence of loyalty and is considered by many to be unethical. You need not approve of everything your supervisor does, but it is best to keep your attitude to yourself.

- Refuse to be influenced by either your supervisor or co-workers to perform unethical acts. A good way to take your stand on any questionable situation is to ask openly: "Is this ethical?"

In summary, building and maintaining a strong, warm, productive relationship with your boss is a real human-relations challenge. It isn't always easy, yet it is an essential step in your progress. You may be used to one supervisor, only to discover that you have been transferred to another department and have to start from scratch. Every relationship will be a unique challenge. Make the most of every experience.

# ◆ CHAPTER 8
## COMMUNICATING AS A TEAM PLAYER

In a previous chapter we took a close look at the various elements often found within a working relationship. We gave recognition to the possible presence of value conflicts, sexual overtones, age differences, and ethnic implications. We introduced the mutual reward theory (MRT) as a way to build and maintain healthy relationships under all conditions.

In this chapter, we focus on how these elements take on more importance for you as a member of a working team.

In the typical traditional department, the supervisor is at the top of the pyramid.

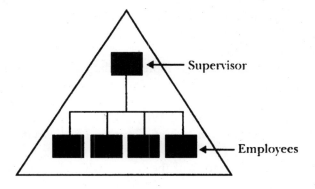

She or he manages or controls the operation from that position, assumes responsibility for results, welcomes suggestions, and often involves employees in decision making, but adheres to the philosophy that *most employees need frequent, steady supervision.*

Under the team concept, the supervisor operates within the team itself.

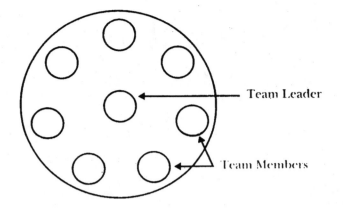

He or she takes time to involve members in the formation of goals, delegates authority and considerable responsibility to the team, communicates frequently, and assumes that team members like to manage themselves.

Anyone who has participated in a team sport learns that success depends upon the contributions of all members. It is one for all and all for one. The pressure to produce comes more from other team members than from the coach. And most important of all is the *way individual members work together*. A good team member is anxious to make another member a star, providing that the team wins. MRT operates at a higher level in a successful team than it does in a traditional department.

The team concept in industry is more popular today than ever before. Entire books have been written on the subject. Experts across the country are offering "team-building" seminars. Many corporations are retraining traditional supervisors to become team leaders. Why all this emphasis*? Because there is evidence that work teams often achieve greater productivity than traditional departments.*

As a potential team member of the future, what should you learn ahead of time so that you can become an outstanding player? Here are three basic requirements:

1. A successful, highly respected team member should accept and promote the four Cs of team membership:

   - Willingness to *conform* to all decisions made by team members.
   - Willingness to *cooperate* with other team members without undue conflict.
   - Willingness to *contribute* talents without holding back for selfish reasons.

- Willingness to *collaborate* with another member on a creative idea, regardless of who receives more recognition for success.

The four Cs communicate how team members can control their behavior so that all actions are in the best interest of the team as a whole. All of this needs to be accomplished with enthusiasm, self-discipline, and little supervision. It is not easy to be a productive member of a work team. Some who have tried it prefer the traditional structure.

2. To be effective, a team must have a leader who is more sensitive to the needs of others—one who can create a working environment where everyone *wants* to contribute. This means that, as a team member, you must understand the role of your team leader and give her or him your full support even when mistakes are made. If you complain about your leader you may also be criticizing your team, which means you are criticizing yourself.

3. Not all work environments are suitable for the team approach. You may be preparing for a career where only parts of the team concept are applicable. For example, fast food operations may have such a fast turnover of personnel that there is not enough time to form a group into a team. In such cases, and many others, the traditional approach may produce the best results. In contrast, in a research department where a high level of creativity is needed, the team approach may be almost mandatory.

Each work environment and situation should be studied by management to determine which approach, the pyramid or the circle—or a blend of both—will produce the best results. Regardless of where you might wind up as an employee, the more you learn about *both* styles the better.

We often hear that the right combination of talent among a team of people can, when everyone is working together, produce a sum greater than the total of each individual operating alone. This is true. Teams that work in harmony (the best possible horizontal relationships) are those that win the awards.

How would you rate yourself as a team member? Completing the exercise that follows may provide you with some insights.

# RATING YOURSELF AS A TEAM MEMBER

The purpose of this exercise is to give you an idea of just how good a team member you might become. Simply place a check mark in the appropriate square opposite each question and total your points at the end. Give an excellent rating 5 points, a good rating 3, and a weak score 1.

| *Question* | *Excellent* | *Good* | *Weak* |
|---|---|---|---|
| 1. How willing would you be to accept the fact that another team member might be stronger than you in a certain area? | ☐ | ☐ | ☐ |
| 2. What would be your chances of maintaining a more positive attitude in a team than working in a regular group or alone? | ☐ | ☐ | ☐ |
| 3. What would be your chances of quickly resolving a human conflict in which you are involved? | ☐ | ☐ | ☐ |
| 4. How good would you be at conforming, cooperating, and contributing when, in some cases, others may enjoy personal gain more than you? | ☐ | ☐ | ☐ |
| 5. What would be your patience threshold in working with a team member slower than yourself? | ☐ | ☐ | ☐ |
| 6. How receptive would you be toward a goal developed by your team when you hold a minority position? | ☐ | ☐ | ☐ |
| 7. How would you rate yourself in terms of working effectively with team members from ethnic groups different from your own? | ☐ | ☐ | ☐ |
| 8. How understanding would you be of members with a point of view different from yours? | ☐ | ☐ | ☐ |
| 9. How well do you think you would accept a team leader who always takes time to see that all members participate in the decision-making process? | ☐ | ☐ | ☐ |
| 10. How successful do you think you might be in keeping your ego from getting in the way of full cooperation with the team? | ☐ | ☐ | ☐ |

TOTAL SCORE

If you scored 40 or more points, you show indications that you would be a sensitive and productive team member. You would probably like being on a team. If you scored between 30 and 40 points, you could probably adjust to team membership without great difficulty. If you scored below 30 points, you might be happier and more productive working in a traditional group or alone.

The next time you are standing in line on a campus, at a bank, or at a post office waiting your turn, study the ethnic diversity of those ahead of you. Recently, I was sixth in line at a post office. A Hispanic mother, a black male, a white teenager, an Asian female, and an East Indian male were ahead of me. This indicates just how culturally diverse some geographical areas in the United States are becoming. I said to myself: "What a challenge it would be to develop a successful team from such a mix of individuals."

There are, of course, teams (and traditional departments) with a low cultural mix:

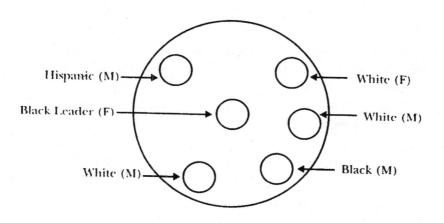

Other teams with a like number of members have a much higher cultural mix:

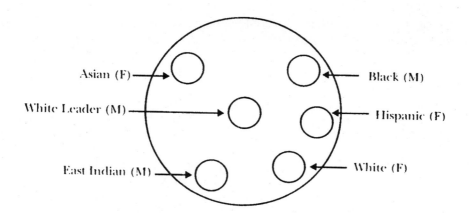

Assume, for a moment, that you are a team member, and a new individual from another culture is assigned to your team. How would you go about helping this individual make the transition? What things might you do to help the new member become comfortable and contribute at a high level? Check those that fall within your comfort zone:

☐ Explain the meaning of some American slang expressions, jargon, or idioms.

☐ In a sensitive way, explain why a mannerism in the person's culture may differ in ours (e.g., handshake vs. a hug).

☐ Discuss little things the newcomer can do to fit more easily into the team and contribute more.

☐ Assist the individual in understanding how workers in our culture deal with leaders and supervisors. For example, explain when and how the newcomer should approach a leader for advice and guidance.

☐ Help the individual understand our business protocol, and be generous in giving compliments when progress is made.

In assisting others to learn our work customs, you will enrich your own life because new employees never forget those who give them a helping hand when they need it most. But there are dangers in overidentifying with new members. Your primary goal should be to strengthen the team, not just build an enjoyable relationship with a person who has an intriguing foreign background. Further, if you go too far, one of two things may happen. First, the newcomer may become overly dependent on you. Second, if you spend too much time with a new team member, you may turn other team members against you.

Although the application of MRT is a successful way to create and maintain harmonious relationships in any environment, its contribution to the success of a work team, when properly understood, can be exceptional. This is because rewards may be unevenly distributed at the beginning, but when the team wins, everything is balanced out. For example, a new team member may need to back up more experienced team members at the start, as in the case of Gregg.

> Gregg was excited when he was invited to join a special team with a great reputation within his company. Experienced members were most helpful during his transition period, but it didn't take them long to discover that Gregg was more interested in his own ideas than in helping others perfect theirs. As a result, he started to isolate himself. Then, to his surprise, a senior member of the team invited him to lunch and said: "Gregg, it is my understanding that you were on the varsity football team in college and that you played the position of guard when your team was in possession of the ball. In short, you did the blocking for your quarterback and those who carried the ball. As a newcomer on our team, your primary job is to block for

others by helping them with their ideas. This doesn't mean you can't carry the ball now and then. You can! And when it happens, others will block for you. Your big job at this point is to help the team become a winner. You see, when the team wins, everyone shares in the rewards. When this happens, it doesn't matter what position you played."

Sometimes new team members forget that when they have an idea that needs support from others, the kind of blocking they receive may depend upon the quality of blocking they did for others when they were new to the team. In the long run, MRT works.

Success as a team member depends heavily upon the attitude of the individual toward the team. All teams are different. They deal with creative matters, production, service, and so on, but no team can function at its highest level if even one member has a consistently negative attitude. Regardless of the type of team, its composition, and its leadership, there are attitude factors that must be present among *all* team members. Here are a few.

- Enthusiastic acceptance of the team concept as an organizational form. This means you support such ideas as supervising yourself and working unselfishly for the team, not because you are expected to contribute your best, but because you *want* to do your best.

- Accepting the four Cs (conforming, cooperating, contributing, and collaborating) because you will achieve more for your firm than would be true if you were an independent worker.

- Undertaking the responsibility of self-discipline because you recognize that your team leader has a less demanding style than would be the case in a traditional department.

- Keeping your own attitude positive and upbeat because you do not want to make it more difficult for other team members.

- Being willing to put your career *temporarily* in the hands of the team. This means that your future is somewhat determined by how other team members perform. Many a professional sports star has had a modest career because he or she was a member of a nonwinning team.

- Realizing that the contributions of other team members may be different from yours, because it is the blending of talent and abilities that can give a team power.

- Maintaining an unprejudiced attitude toward all team members, regardless of cultural and other differences.

- Realizing that a good team leader probably has some of the attributes of a successful coach and that your attitude toward this key individual is crucial.

Anyone who has been a member of a sports team of any kind probably has some valuable insights into what makes a work team successful. The more these insights are applied, the better. The comparison, however, can only go so far. Sports teams operate for only one season, then they can start over with some new members and a built-in goal of winning a conference. A work team, on the other hand, does not have the luxury of starting over frequently. Not only that, but an organizational team must create goals from within and provide its own rewards. The thrill of winning, however, can be equally satisfying.

# ◆PART THREE

---

## ORGANIZATIONAL COMMUNICATION
## AS A WAY OF COPING

---

Effective organizational communication and human relations depend on the knowledge and skills (competence) of managers and employees. The purpose of Part Three of this book is to discuss the challenging situations people often face at work and to suggest ways managers and employees can choose communication and human relations strategies appropriate to those situations.

Part Three provides a useful starting point for dealing with some of the most difficult situations people face at work—frustration, anger, injured relationships, organizational testing, and conflict. The main idea is that these challenging events take place in *communicative situations*. "Communicative situations" are where communication behaviors are required to "cope" with the conditions that people perceive to exist around them, as opposed to "managing," which attempts to direct or control events.

## ◆ THE COMMUNICATIVE SITUATION

In 1970, communication theorist Lloyd Bitzer coined the phrase "rhetorical situation." "Rhetoric" is a kind of purposeful communication, which takes place in particular kinds of settings, and is usually associated with persuasion. In fact, the ancient Greek philosopher Aristotle defined rhetoric as using all the available means of persuasion. Rhetorical information does not emphasize expressing feelings or presenting information, but uses emotion and information to change people's minds.

Bitzer defined his rhetorical situation as having three characteristics—a *challenge,* problem, or obstacle; an *audience* of people who are capable of having their minds changed and helping to implement the desired changes, meaning that the speaker has some "leverage" with them; and *constraints* that limit the range of available communication strategies and restrict the persuader's ability to affect the situation and change minds, such as beliefs, attitudes, human relations skills, and power. The three characteristics combine to form the context or climate within which communication choices are made.

We choose to identify the situation Bitzer described as "communicative" because we want to downplay the purposeful or rhetorical part of it, and highlight the relational and responsive elements (see the concepts of relational communication in Chapter 2 and "responding" to conflict in Chapter 12).

The idea we want to emphasize is that we do not so much control or manage situations like stress and conflict as we need to cope with those situations. We think it's an important distinction.

---

*To manage can imply changing or manipulating the*
*world around you; to cope is intended to imply*
*that changes need to happen within you.*

---

# ◆ COPING WITH ORGANIZATIONAL CHALLENGES

Whenever we face a challenge like stress, conflict, or a poor working relationship in a communicative situation, choosing an appropriate response or way to cope is difficult. Communicative situations sometimes paralyze an employee. Sometimes the challenge or problem is clear, sometimes it is not. The problem can be clear, but the constraints are not. Often employees and managers have no guidelines for coping with difficult organizational situations.

*Many organizations gives their employees very little structure or guidelines for coping with challenging communicative situations.*

For example, telling a manager "to relax" or an employee "to work it out" with a disagreeable co-worker provides few practical guidelines for making meaningful choices. Without some sense of what directions to pursue, employees are left to rely on their own devices. This, in and of itself, can be a tremendous source of frustration and stress.

Organizations often place their employees in difficult situations with no productive way to respond. They create challenges that require action, but also create constraints that leave little room for productive courses of action or choice.

But like the rest of this book, the chapters in this part assume that the ability to cope with communicative situations also depends on the level of an employee's attitudes and skills—in other words, the employee's communication competence (see Chapter 4). The level of competence—knowledge and performance—either gives the employee a wide range of potential coping strategies or reduces the available choices. A full repertoire of knowledge about various communication ideas may allow a person to see constraints that he or she might otherwise overlook, thereby suggesting guidelines for appropriate communication performance in difficult situations.

*It is the combination of organizational factors and individual competence that makes the lives of employees frustrating or productive.*

Successful employees learn to cope with complicated situations because they develop effective communication and human relations skills. They have the competence to understand how personal and organizational factors limit their freedom to choose. They have the competence to see how organizational situations are matrices of communicative situations, challenges, audiences, and constraints.

# ◆ THE PURPOSE OF PART THREE OF THE BOOK

The purpose of the chapters in Part Three of this book is *to help you increase competence in coping with difficult communicative situations at work by suggesting concepts for making sense of those situations and behaviors for practice.*

    Chapter 9 will discuss the relationship between frustration and aggression and suggest ways for communicating through frustration effectively. Chapter 10 will look at effective ways for coping with an injured working relationship.

    Chapter 11 emphasizes the attitudes and skills necessary to cope with teasing and organizational testing. Chapter 12 concludes Part Three with a discussion regarding communicating through organizational conflict. It offers a perspective that says conflict happens by way of communication and is coped with or not through both effective command and relational communication.

# ◆ CHAPTER 9

## COMMUNICATING YOUR FRUSTRATIONS HARMLESSLY

The purpose of this chapter is to introduce you to the frustration–aggression hypothesis. It is an idea that can greatly assist you in understanding your own communication behavior and that of others. Here is the story.

Everyone encounters frustrations in life. We learn to adjust to most of them easily, without hurting our relations with others. Sometimes, however, a major frustration or series of frustrations may cause our feelings to boil to the point where we lash out verbally and seriously injure or destroy a relationship we deeply treasure.

Naturally many disturbing experiences occur on the job. In fact, most of your frustrations may be job related. The mechanic who climbs under a car to do a repair job, only to discover that he or she brought the wrong wrench, becomes frustrated. A supervisor who must get a report in before going home to an important dinner engagement must deal with feelings of frustration.

---

*Frustration is the feeling of disturbance or anxiety you experience when you meet a temporary block to your immediate goal.*

---

The more important the goal is to you, the more intense is the disturbance. Major frustrations come about when something happens to keep you from reaching a goal that means a great deal to you. While small frustrations can usually be dealt with quickly, major frustrations must often be controlled for days or weeks before an adjustment can be made. This often means replacing one goal with another.

Now we must ask ourselves the big question: What happens when we become frustrated?

*Almost always we become aggressive.* When a steam boiler builds up too much pressure inside, some of the steam must be released. If there is no safety valve, the boiler will explode. Just as the steam boiler must release some of the pressure after it reaches a certain point, so must the individual. This release usually comes in some form of aggressive behavior.

Take the case of the driver who becomes frustrated when he (or she) meets a slow-moving car on the highway. He may curse (verbal aggression) and drive on. Or he may pound his horn and speed around the slow car (physical aggression). Or it could disturb him so much that when he returns to his office he may refuse to speak to his secretary or co-workers (passive aggression).

Aggression takes many forms. Physical aggression, especially if it involves another person, is serious. It can be assault and battery and could mean a police record. Verbal aggression can also get a person into serious trouble. Telling off a fellow worker or supervisor at the wrong time and place can destroy a relationship and cripple a person's progress.

*The idea is to learn to communicate our aggression in acceptable ways without hurting our relationships with others.* There are acceptable forms of physical aggression. There are acceptable forms of verbal aggression.

A parent might become frustrated because of her (or his) small children. She could act out the aggression that follows the frustration by punishing one child with a very harsh slap in the face. This is an unacceptable release of aggression. On the other hand, if she released her aggression physically by energetically washing windows, and then disciplined the child in some other manner, it would be more acceptable. This way the mother is taking out her aggression on the windows—not on the child.

There are many acceptable ways a person can release inner tension due to frustrations. Here are a few.

| **On the Job** | **Off the Job** |
| --- | --- |
| Take a walk | Cook exotic foods |
| Talk things over with a third party | Clean out the garage |
| Do some disagreeable stock work | Play golf or go bowling |

Sometimes just by doing something physical we release inner tensions and no one is hurt. It is usually more difficult to find acceptable ways to release inner tensions on the job than it is off the job.

If a worker became frustrated on the job and picked a fight with a fellow worker, this would be an unacceptable release of aggression. If, on the other hand, he (or she) walked away and slammed a door where nobody could hear it, he would be releasing his aggression in an acceptable manner. He *could* hurt his human relationships, however, by slamming a door in *front* of others. They might interpret the action as a display of temper or immaturity.

As a mature, mentally healthy person, you must seek and find acceptable releases for your inner aggression. You should conduct yourself in such a manner as to eliminate many of the frustrations of life. The fewer frustrations you have, the fewer times you will have to seek acceptable releases.

But you cannot eliminate all frustrations from life. You should expect to find it necessary to release your anxiety feelings occasionally. It is not always healthy for a person to keep his or her tensions bottled up. Some release is necessary and healthy. You would do well, however, to refrain from any kind of verbal aggression on the job. It would be wiser to unburden yourself to someone you can trust outside the organization—your spouse or a good friend.

Here is an illustration that will help you to understand the importance of the frustration–aggression hypothesis.

Alice was intelligent, highly motivated, and well educated. She joined a large utility company as a management trainee. She liked her job, and for two years her productivity and human relations were very good. She took advantage of every opportunity to learn. She received four salary increases.

One day, in talking to the director of human resources, she mentioned that she would like to qualify as an employment interviewer. The director, pleased with her success so far, encouraged her. He told Alice that she would be considered if an opportunity came along. Alice, more highly motivated than ever, continued to do an outstanding job and set her goal for the next opening as an interviewer.

Two weeks later another person was promoted to the position of interviewer. Alice was not informed about the change. Not thinking that the plans for this personnel change might have been set before her initial talk with the director, Alice permitted herself to become deeply frustrated. She had set a goal for herself, and now they had selected another person.

"At least they could have talked to me!"

"Why should that person get the breaks?"

"So that's the way they keep their promises!"

Alice, without thinking it through, permitted her frustration to grow. Indeed, she set out to feed it, for talking it over with a few fellow employees only intensified her feelings.

What happened?

Alice released her frustrations through verbal aggression. For the first time in her career, she sounded off in a highly emotional manner at a weekly staff meeting. She voiced more than her share of gripes during coffee breaks. And all of this found its way back to the department of human resources. What was the result? What you might expect: Alice, through her verbal aggression, had hurt her previously excellent relationship with others. Six months later another position as an interviewer opened up, and Alice was passed over.

What should she have done?

Alice should have released her aggressive behavior outside her job until she discovered the truth of the situation. She could have spent more time playing her favorite sport or talking her problem over with a close friend. Or she could have vented her frustration by putting it into writing without showing it to others. This seems to help a number of people. None of these actions would have injured her relations with others.

We must all learn to live with frustrating experiences without becoming verbally aggressive on the job, without damaging our relations with others, and *without victimizing ourselves.*

Aggressive behavior resulting from inner disturbances and hostilities takes many strange forms. It's not always physical or verbal—it may be passive. In extreme cases, passive aggression takes the form of silence—deliberate silence, planned silence.

Silence on the part of the person who has been frustrated is a most potent weapon. Nothing is more uncomfortable to your fellow workers than your silence. Nothing destroys relations faster. No one can interpret your silence. All anyone can do is to leave you alone and wait. But it is uncomfortable for them, and productivity suffers.

When a person takes out his or her inner aggressive feelings in silence, who is on the receiving end? Fellow employees? The supervisor? Although everyone suffers from silence of this nature, the silent person himself suffers the most. He is, in fact, taking out his aggressive feelings on himself. It is a form of self-victimization. Naturally, this is most destructive to the human personality. It is also juvenile. Many normal, mature people, however, temporarily react to a series of frustrations in this manner.

It is hoped that the preceding discussion has given you a good understanding of the frustration–aggression hypothesis. To summarize, how can you put this idea to work for you?

1. If you really understand the idea, you will admit that your frustrations often produce aggressive behavior of some kind and that you should learn to recognize this. With this recognition should come the ability to channel aggressive actions into acceptable outlets. Be careful to release your aggressions in the right way and in the right place. Keep from releasing them on the job in a way that will hurt relationships and your future.

2. You should be able to recognize aggressive behavior in others (including executives). This should help you remember that aggressive action by others is usually not directed toward you personally. You may just happen to be at the wrong place at the wrong time and the best available target for verbal abuse. You should try to accept such behavior as a natural outcome of uncontrollable frustrations and not overreact to it. This attitude should make for better human understanding. Your relationship with this person will not suffer as much.

3. You should be more sensitive to verbal aggression on your own part, and be very cautious in group discussions and staff meetings. When you need to release feelings verbally, do so to a friend outside the company and not to a fellow employee, thus protecting your work relationships.

**4.** You should not let aggressive behavior keep you from reaching your ultimate goal. When a detour is necessary, you should take it. When an unexpected block to your plans appears, accept it for what it is. If frustration occurs, release it in acceptable ways and come up with an alternative goal. Do not allow aggressive behavior to victimize you on a permanent basis.

There is another form of aggression that should be mentioned. It is subtle and sinister and has been the downfall of many career-minded persons. It is aggression on the part of an employee toward the company for which he or she works. There is rarely anything personal about such a person's aggressive behavior. Such a person seems to get along well enough with fellow workers and immediate supervisors. Instead, the aggression always seems to be directed toward the company itself. It isn't just the top brass or middle management—it is the company. The employee often seems to hold his or her present plight (lack of progress or of personal adjustment to life) against the company.

In a very real sense, it is frustrating to work in any organization. Some rules must be followed. Some degree of conformity is expected. Some loss of individuality is usually necessary. Some people, however, seem to nurse their minor frustrations into one major hang-up against the organization itself. When this is permitted to happen, aggressive action of serious proportions frequently develops. The employee begins to fight a hypothetical monster that seems to be controlling his or her life without giving the person a chance to change. Often one hears expressions like these from such an individual:

"This outfit does nothing but chew people up and spit them out."

"This company is so large that the only thing that keeps us from getting lost altogether is the computer."

"I'd put in for a transfer, but by the time it got through channels I'd be ready to retire."

It is counterproductive to direct one's aggressive behavior toward a large corporate structure. In the first place, these organizations are usually too large. Second, when a person attacks the company, he or she starts to lose loyalty to it. *And it begins to show in the employee's attitude*—not overnight, of course, but in subtle ways that begin to hurt that person's progress in the company.

View stress as the fever that comes with overwork, trying to reach too many goals at the same time, and dealing with difficult peers and superiors. When you learn to release your frustrations harmlessly, you are lowering the fever by reducing the stress that has accumulated within you. For example, assume that you build the stress within you to a level where action is required. What do you do? You release the stress through some form of activity, recreation, or just getting away for a short time. This lowers the fever. Then, by rebuilding yourself physically (through more activity), you also recover your positive attitude. In other words, one answer to burnout is managing stress by releasing your frustrations without having to cut back on your productivity.

This chapter has attempted to show you why you should try to communicate your frustrations harmlessly. Its purpose has been to help you avoid self-victimization so that you maintain the positive, productive relationship that will further, not hinder, your career progress.

# ◆CHAPTER 10
## COMMUNICATION AND
## INJURED RELATIONSHIPS

No matter how skillful one becomes at building healthy and rewarding human relationships, such relationships can easily be damaged through insensitivity and misunderstanding by either party. Human relationships are fragile. Once an injury occurs, the restoration process can be like walking on glass barefooted; it can be difficult—even challenging—but not impossible.

In the work environment, damages occur when there is a misuse of power by leaders, when the behavior of one party toward another is less than honest, when there are breakdowns in communications, and for a host of other reasons, many of which are highly personal and unintended. The important thing to remember is that *all* relationships—both on and off the job—occasionally become damaged and need repairing. When repair work is required and nothing is done about it, everyone loses. That is why it could be to your advantage to initiate restoration *even when you are not primarily responsible for the injury.*

Without intending to do so, June let her emotions spill over last Friday and became testy with Grace, her favorite co-worker. Grace, wounded emotionally, reacted with a huffy silence for the rest of the day. June worried about the situation all weekend but failed to make repairs Monday. Early Tuesday, Grace initiated a discussion on the incident that gave June an opportunity to apologize, and the relationship was restored. Although she was not at fault, Grace was not content to work under an uncomfortable climate, so she used her human-relations skills to restore the relationship.

Last week Gilbert came down too hard on Harry over a minor work rule infraction. Harry, knowing Gilbert (his supervisor) would find it difficult to apologize, took action himself. On the following day he said: "Gilbert, our relationship is important to me, so I want to keep communication lines open and eliminate any differences that may occur between us. I want to be relaxed and comfortable under your supervision. Is it a deal?"

Unfortunately, when a minor falling out between two people occurs, both parties may have a desire to nurse the hurt and pull further away from each other. If this is allowed to continue, some dangerous side effects may develop. For example, the possibility exists that the relationship between them may become more "toxic" and spill over into bad relationships with others.

> The rift that developed between Jill and Jessie pushed Jill into a negative rut where some of her other relationships seemed to turn sour. The cause? A change in attitude. Jill started to ask herself such questions as: "Why should I work hard to build healthy relationships when others couldn't care less?" "Why should I permit myself to be vulnerable to the hurts of others carelessly imposed upon me?" The result? Jill withdrew into her newly designed shell and became less of a team member on the job and less socially accepted in her personal world. Jill had made the classic human relations mistake of permitting a repairable rift to develop into a major problem.

If communication is the lifeblood of any relationship, then reopening communication lines should be the first step in restoring relationships. Which party initiates the communication is unimportant. Communication, in this sense, can be compared to using ointment to help heal a cut. The ointment (communication) by itself may not solve the problem, but it enhances the healing process. If neither party is willing to supply or apply the ointment, the wound may fester and eventually destroy the relationship.

Regardless of who may be at fault (often both parties are responsible), it is effective human-relations practice to restore the relationship *as soon as possible.* Any lapse of time may seem to deaden the pain, but it can make restoration more difficult—and sometimes impossible. And those who move from one job to another, leaving a wake of broken relationships behind them, often pay a high price in many directions. Consider the following possibilities.

*Constructive "mind time" is lost.* Preoccupation with a relationship left unrepaired is self-defeating. Living day in and day out with an unhealthy relationship, especially with a supervisor, causes you to mentally reprocess the conflict over and over, thus stealing your "mind time" from more constructive pursuits. Those who permit this to happen often put their career progress on hold or in jeopardy.

*An already stressful situation is compounded.* Emotional conflicts in the workplace can be more stressful than long hours, heavy concentration on a special project, or other heavy job demands. Worst of all, emotional stress makes everything else more difficult. To maintain peace of mind and high personal productivity, restoration of broken relationships should receive top priority. When this is not done, false inferences often compound the stress. For years statistics have indicated that more than 50 percent of all resignations come from unsolved human conflicts.

*Chances of becoming a victim increase.* In some work environments, a broken relationship left unattended can convert you into a victim. For example, a co-worker with whom you previously enjoyed a healthy relationship suddenly begins to fear you may replace him or her. As a result, this individual deliberately creates a conflict situation in the hope that you will be unable to deal with it effectively. If the supervisor does not step in as a mediator/counselor, and you refuse to take action yourself, you could easily wind up a victim. Your refusal to take action (even going to the supervisor with the problem) could give the co-worker the upper hand he or she seeks, and eventually management could misinterpret the situation in favor of the other party. Your failure to remove the feeling of fear through communication and restore the relationship to its previous state could cause you to become a victim.

Such possibilities, although remote, should motivate you to set the difficult goal of creating, maintaining, and repairing relationships, even when you would prefer to ignore the individuals involved or carry out a vendetta against them. In some cases, your career may depend upon how effective you are.

There are four principles or guideposts that may assist you in repairing a damaged relationship.

1. *See the connection between repairing relationships and career success.* A damaged relationship left unrepaired between you and a co-worker or superior may reduce support you need at a later date. As a result, your upward mobility may be impeded. You have victimized yourself.

2. *Try to see behind the cause of the falling out.* When one takes the time to study the causes of breaks in human relationships, it becomes obvious that often one party was under unusual pressure, which precipitated the rift. It is easier to forgive when such causes can be identified. Through your own perception, try to see behind misunderstandings. Once you see why they occur, your attitude toward rebuilding them may be more positive.

3. *Develop a willingness to rebuild damaged relationships.* The more you nurse a resentment, the less effective you are in restoring a relationship. Some give-and-take from both ends is usually necessary for a satisfactory repair job. If one party is unwilling to listen, the process may never get off the ground. That is why some relationships are never repaired. Until you reach a point where your mind is open to the possibility of repair (regardless of who did the damage), you have not reached the effective level of *willingness*.

4. *Design your own rebuilding techniques.* As you ponder just how you might initiate a rebuilding process, many questions will emerge. Can both parties save face? If hostility and resentment are present, can they be dissipated through open communication so that the repair job is permanent? As you consider such factors, ask yourself these additional questions:

   Can you insert some humor into your approach?

   Can you be a better listener than a talker?

   Can you "give" as much as you expect from the other party?

   Can you forgive a little white lie so that the other party can save face?

Are you willing to state openly that the relationship is important to you—important enough to forgive and forget what or who caused the damage?

Once you feel your "willingness factor" is sufficient, consider these rebuilding strategies:

*Rebuilding strategy 1:* If you were fully or partially responsible for the damage, swallow your pride and take the direct approach. Say you are sorry and state: "I would like to get our relationship back to its previous healthy state as soon as possible. You and our relationship are important to me, and I intend to be more sensitive in the future."

We all make human-relations mistakes. We always will. Unless we accept the premise that now and then we need to initiate a repair job, we will lose many significant relationships well worth keeping.

*Rebuilding strategy 2:* When the party at the other end of the relationship line makes the mistake (the reason is not important), give that party the opportunity to approach you to restore the relationship. Be accessible! Have an open mind! If the party does not approach you in a reasonable length of time, take the initiative yourself. This may sound like asking too much, but keep in mind that you may be getting hurt more than the person responsible. Why should you become a victim? Why not restore the relationship for *your* benefits? One way to employ strategy 2 is to say: "That incident last week really got to me, Jack, and I'm bringing it up for discussion so that hopefully it won't happen again. If we don't work harder at maintaining our relationship, we will both wind up losers."

*Rebuilding strategy 3:* When no one is clearly responsible for a rift, initiate an MRT discussion so that the rewards parties are receiving from the relationship can be reviewed. This approach can help each party recognize how important the relationship has been in the past and can continue to be in the future. Only when rewards are somewhat equal do both parties come out ahead. That is the significance and the promise of MRT.

Restoring a damaged relationship involves risks. You may, for example, gather up your courage in a sincere effort to restore an important relationship, only to be rebuffed for your initiative.

After two days of increased silence and tension on the job, Howard approached his boss to reconcile a communications misunderstanding. His boss responded by walking away. However, the following morning Howard's boss invited him to lunch, and the relationship was fully restored. With time to think over Howard's gesture, his boss had a change of attitude. The risk had been worth taking after all.

*Some people refuse to restore a relationship even if the alternative means finding a new job.* Yet the challenge of restoration can be rich and rewarding and, at times, can give a career a needed boost.

In conclusion, keep in mind that a professional technician needs just the right tool to repair a sensitive instrument. The right tool to repair a damaged relationship is communication—in fact, it is the *only* tool available. When you use communication in a sensitive manner, you will be more than pleased with your repair jobs.

# ◆ CHAPTER 11
## COPING WITH ORGANIZATIONAL TESTING

Getting started in a new job or assignment, where the setting is strange and the employees are strangers, is bound to give you a few psychological challenges. It is not my purpose to magnify these. Rather, we wish to help you understand why such problems sometimes develop—and, even more important, show you how you can handle them.

You may be assigned to a department as a replacement for someone the others hated to lose. They will need time to get used to you. You may not have the experience of the person you replace and, as a result, others may have to work harder for a few days to get you started. It is even possible that someone in your new department wanted another person to have your job, and there may be some resentment toward you because of this.

It is never easy to be the newest member of a group. You cannot expect to go from being an outsider to being an insider without making a few adjustments. In the first place, you and your personality were forced upon the group. They were not asked whether they wanted you. You have been, in effect, imposed upon them. Because they were there first, and because they probably have strong relationships among themselves, they may feel that you should earn your way into their confidence. It may not seem fair, but it is only natural for them to look at your arrival in this way.

Did you ever go through an initiation into a club? If so, you will understand that teasing or testing the new member is often traditional. To a limited extent, the same can be true when a new employee joins a department or division in a business organization. There is nothing planned or formal about it, of course, but you should be prepared for a little good-natured teasing or testing. Let us look at the psychological reasons behind these two phenomena.

## ◆ TEASING

The teasing of a new employee is often nothing more than a way of helping the person become a full-fledged member of the group. It is a form of initiation rite that will help you feel you belong. Sometimes it is a group effort in which everyone is in on the joke. More often, however, it is an individual matter.

---

*Teasing, for the most part, is harmless.*

---

The shop foreman who never had the advantage of a college education but who has learned a great deal from practical experience might enjoy teasing a recent graduate of an engineering school. If the graduate engineer goes along with the teasing, a sound relationship between the two should develop. If, however, she or he permits it to get under her skin, the relationship could become strained.

The shop foreman's motive might be nothing more than a desire to help the new engineer build good relationships with the rest of the gang. There may be nothing resentful or personal about it.

A small group of employees who work together closely in a branch bank, lawyer's office, or similar situation can usually be expected to come up with a little harmless teasing when a new person joins the staff. He might be given the oldest equipment with a touch of formal ceremony or the dismal job of keeping the stockroom in order.

Usually this kind of teasing is based upon tradition and human nature. People who like to tease in this manner are generally good-natured. They enjoy people. They mean no harm. In fact, they usually do it to make you feel more comfortable, not less.

If you are on the receiving end of some good, healthy teasing, you have nothing to worry about so long as you don't take it personally. Just go along with it and you'll come out ahead. It is much better to be teased than to be ignored. If by chance the baiting should go a little too far and you find yourself embarrassed, the very fact that it is embarrassing to you will probably make you some friends. In fact, you will be lucky if there is some mild hazing. It will help you get off to a good start. It will help break down any communications barriers that might exist.

## ◆ TESTING

Testing is different. It can have more serious implications. It will take more understanding on your part.

There are two kinds of testing. One is *organizational testing*. This kind comes from the organization (management, personnel, or your supervisor) and is a deliberate attempt to discover what kind of person you really are and whether you can adjust to certain conditions. The other kind comes strictly from individuals. This is *personal testing*—one person trying out another because of personality conflicts or inner prejudices.

# ◆ ORGANIZATIONAL TESTING

Almost all kinds of organizations—especially the smaller ones—have certain unpleasant tasks that must be done. Traditionally, these tasks are handed to the newest member. The new salesperson in a department store may be given excessive amounts of stock work at the start of his or her career. The factory worker may be given unpleasant cleanup jobs until another new member joins the department. The clerical employee may be given a nasty filing assignment to start with.

The important thing to recognize is that these tests have a purpose. Can the new worker take the assignment without complaining? Can he or she survive without developing a negative attitude? Or will this person show resentment and thereby destroy his or her chance of gaining the respect of the other members of the department?

The old phrase "starting at the bottom of the ladder" sometimes means exactly that. Many top management people started at the bottom, and they feel that this is the best way for you to start. If you can't take it to begin with, you may not be able to assume heavy responsibility later. It is the price you pay for being a beginner.

Management sometimes feels that this is the best way for the manager of the future to appreciate fully the kind of work that must be done by the rank-and-file employee. Many college graduates find themselves doing the most uninviting tasks to start with. If they are human-relations smart, they will take it in stride, using the time to size up the situation and learn as much about the organization as possible.

During testing periods you are being watched by management and by your fellow employees. *The better you react, the sooner the testing will end and the better your relations with others will be.* In other words, although getting the job done is important, your attitude toward it may be more important. If you react in a negative manner, three things can happen: 1) you may be kept on the assignment longer than you otherwise would have been, 2) you may hurt your chances of getting a better assignment later on, and 3) you may damage relationships with people involved in or observing the testing.

If you can take the long-range perspective and condition yourself to these tasks with an inner smile and an outward grin, you'll do well for yourself. Roll up your sleeves and get the job done quickly. If you finish one job, move on to another. Don't be afraid to get dirty. If you must take a little abuse, don't complain. It is part of the initiation rite, and you will look back on it someday as those ahead of you look back on it now. It would be foolhardy for the new employee to fight any of the many forms of organizational testing, as long as it doesn't seriously damage his or her personal dignity.

# ◆ PERSONAL TESTING

Personal testing is a different matter. It could give you more trouble, especially if you fail to recognize it for what it is. It may come from someone your own age or someone much older or younger. It may come from a fellow worker or from someone in management. You might be wise to start out with the attitude that everything is teasing rather than testing. Then, if it doesn't last long, you have automatically solved the problem.

But if the teasing continues for a long period of time, you will know that it is personal testing and that it is probably the product of genuine hostility. When this happens, you have a real challenge ahead of you. For example, one of your fellow employees may refuse to accept you. He or she may harass you at every turn and may not give you a chance to be a normal, productive employee. The needle will be out at every opportunity.

### Serious Testing #1

Ray had this experience when he was assigned to a maintenance crew with a gas and water company. The job was extremely important to him because it had taken him a long time to get it. He also knew that he was on a very strict ninety-day probation period. Because of this, Ray decided that he would go all out to keep his personal productivity high and still build good relationships with the rest of the crew.

Everything would have been great if it had not been for Art, who started out the very first day using every technique in the book to slow Ray down and get under his skin. Art constantly came up with comments like "What are you trying to do, Ray, make us all look bad?" "Who are you kissin' up to by working so hard?" "If you slow down a little, kid, we'll get you through probation."

After three weeks of this, Ray knew he was up against a personality conflict loaded with hostility. Rather than take it any longer, he invited Art to have coffee with him after work one day. It was a strained evening, but Art finally relaxed. Much of the hostility disappeared, and the next day he was off Ray's back. Ray never discovered the real cause of the conflict. The crew seemed happier, and productivity was better.

Chances are good that it will never happen to you personally, but occasionally an employee will get on the receiving end of some nonorganizational or personal testing from a supervisor. This is what happened to both Rachel and Jess.

### Serious Testing #2

Rachel, a young black woman, graduated near the top of her class in nursing school. She took the first job she interviewed for as a vocational nurse in a large nursing home for elderly people. But Rachel quickly discovered that she was on the receiving end of some rather vicious testing from her supervisor.

She was not surprised when she received a lot of ugly jobs during her first few days. She knew it was traditional, so she pleasantly went about giving baths to some of the most difficult patients. She had many disagreeable duties, all of which were assigned to her by the supervisor, a registered nurse who had been at the home for many years.

Rachel didn't complain; she didn't want any special favors because she was black. She took everything that came her way because she wanted to prove to herself that she could take it. But slowly she began to sense that something more than routine testing was involved. Her supervisor seemed to dish out the ugly assignments with a strange, subtle bitterness. Not only that, but even after two new vocational nurses had joined the staff, Rachel was still doing all the really dirty jobs.

Although she was fearful of racial prejudice from the beginning, she tried to play it cool and hope for a change. She said nothing. But soon her fellow workers, most of whom were her age and also vocational nurses, got the message. When they did, a confrontation took place that finally reached the desk of the owner. The pressure on Rachel was quickly removed, and no one was sorry a week later when the registered nurse responsible resigned.

It is sometimes impossible to know the deep-seated motives behind some of the serious testing that takes place. Often the people responsible do not know themselves. Racial prejudice is only one of the many causes, as the case involving Mario will illustrate.

**Serious Testing #3**

Mario was really pleased about his new construction job. At last he would be able to put his apprenticeship training to work and make some good money. He anticipated all the teasing he got from the old-timers at the beginning, and he took it in stride without any big scenes. But his foreman's attitude was something else. No matter how hard he tried, Mario got the needle from his foreman at every turn. No matter how much work Mario turned out, the foreman was on his back. Mario took it for about a week, and then, in desperation, he asked the advice of one of the older crew members. Here is what the older man said: "Look, buddy, our beloved supervisor is an uptight conservative. Your long hair, your flashy sports car, and especially your free and easy lifestyle all get to him. Frankly, I think he has some trouble with his own sons, and you remind him of them. At any rate, he's all wrong. What you do to get him off your back, though, is your own problem. Good luck."

Mario gave it some serious thought and decided that he would face the foreman and see what happened. It was a tough decision to make because he didn't want to lose his job. He waited until they were alone, and then he put all his cards on the table. He said, "You've been on my back and you know it. I think you should either tell me why or start treating me the way you treat the others." There were some tense and awkward moments, but when it was all over the foreman managed a small smile, and from then on things were noticeably better for Mario.

These three examples represent only a few of the many different cases that could be presented. Sometimes sexual harassment is involved. Sometimes supervisors are responsible, sometimes they are not. The question is, of course, what can you do if you come up against a serious testing situation?

Here are a few pointers that may help you.

Accept the situation willingly until you have time to analyze it carefully. Take it as part of the test period and conduct yourself in such a manner as not to aggravate the situation. It may pass by itself, or someone else, without your knowledge, may come to your rescue. If time does not take care of it and you come to the point where you sincerely feel that you are being pushed too far, approach the person who is doing the needling with a "let's lay all the cards on the table" attitude. In your own words, without hostility, say something like this: "If I have done anything to upset you, please tell me. Otherwise, I feel it is time we started to respect each other."

This will not be easy for you to do. But in cases of extreme testing, it is necessary to make the tester account for his or her actions. There is no other solution.

Unfortunately, some individuals will push you around indefinitely if you permit it. And if you permit it, they will never respect you. Chances are that this will not happen to you, but if it does, you must stand up to the situation and solve it yourself. It is important to you and to the company that you do so.

Of course, you need to go about it in the right way. Try not to have a chip on your shoulder. Do not make accusations. Try not to say anything personal about the man or woman you are standing up to. Your goal is to open up the relationship, to find a foundation upon which you can build for the future. Your goal is to demolish the psychological barrier, not to find out who is responsible for it. You must make it easy for the other person to save face. In most cases of testing (even when a healthy relationship has yet to be built), the principles and techniques found in Chapter 12 are applicable, and it may be helpful to consider them.

Unless the testing is extremely severe or prolonged, you may be better off not going to others, either inside or outside your organization, for help. You will be respected for taking care of the problem yourself. If, however, you have made every effort to clear it up over a reasonable length of time and you have had no success, you should go to your supervisor and discuss it honestly and freely. Situations of this kind should not be permitted to continue to the point where departmental morale and productivity are impaired.

If you can prove that discrimination or sexual harassment is involved, you should feel free to take your case to your local Fair Practices Labor Board.

It is important not to anticipate such situations—they are very rare. Such a problem may never come your way. For the most part, teasing and testing will be good-natured—maybe even enjoyable—if you have the right attitude.

# ◆CHAPTER 12

## COMUNICATING EFFECTIVELY THROUGH ORGANIZATIONAL CONFLICT

Fighting, hostility, and controversy are nearly everyday fare for individuals and groups in organizational settings. Disagreement and conflict are inevitable aspects of working relationships, and the need to communicate effectively in conflict situations is always with us.

For many years, organizational theorists viewed conflict as inherently negative. Conflicts were seen as revealing a weakness in the organization—a flaw in its design, operation, and communication processes. Conflict was something to be "resolved." Sources of conflict had to be identified and eliminated as soon as possible. Peace and stability had to be returned to the organization.

The view of conflict in this chapter is quite different. We emphasize that organizational conflicts are neither inherently negative nor positive, although they do vary in their productiveness and destructiveness. Conflicts that are relatively productive for getting a job done may be highly destructive for a particular employee. Similarly, conflicts that are damaging to getting tasks accomplished may be advantageous for an employee.

---

*As a form of organizational communication, any conflict is about both tasks (commands) and people (relations).*

---

The focus of this chapter is to help you effectively communicate through events that are the concrete manifestations of organizational conflict. Conflict happens by way of communication and is coped with (or not) through both command and relational communication. Consequently, if you want to cope effectively with the conflict, you have to look at it as requiring effective communication attitudes and skills. While all conflict is not rooted in poor communication, it always involves communication attitudes and skills.

Organizational conflicts can be communicated through effectively by looking at three key areas: 1) What is organizational conflict and how does it work, including its benefits? 2) What are the different types of organizational conflict? 3) What can employees and managers do about each type?

# ◆ DEFINING ORGANIZATIONAL CONFLICT AS COMMUNICATION

A few years ago, the American Management Association sponsored a survey of managerial interests in the area of conflict. The respondents in the survey were 116 chief executives, 76 vice presidents, and 66 middle managers. The survey strongly suggested that organizational conflict is a topic of growing importance:

- Managers spend about 24 percent of their time dealing with conflict.
- Conflict management is an increasingly important skill for managers.
- Conflict management skills are rated as equal or more important than planning, motivational, and decision-making skills.
- Communication is a source of conflict.

But these executives and managers also revealed what they considered to be the principle causes of organizational conflict. Among the described causes were:

- Communication failure
- Personality clashes
- Value and goal differences
- Substandard performances
- Differences over method
- Responsibility issues
- Competition for limited resources

Clearly, two important inferences can be drawn from the study. One, conflict is a growing reality of organizational life. Second, it's difficult for managers to get a handle on the complex dynamics of conflict. Grounds for conflict exist whenever people are involved in *interdependent* and *interactive* relationships. When employees' roles are interdependent, there are many situations over which conflicts can arise.

We believe the initial step in "handling" conflict, or as we prefer to put it, *communicating effectively through conflict situations,* is to know what conflict is and how it works. Once you've made some sense out of conflict and its communication dynamics, you are better able to figure out what you can do about it. We now offer a communication-oriented definition of conflict that suggests specific ways for communicating through conflict situations. Many of the ideas in this chapter come from John Stewart's and Virginia Satir's writings on communication and interpersonal relations.

We agree with Stewart, who defines "conflict" as *verbally and nonverbally expressed disagreement between individuals or groups in an organization.* Though broad, his definition allows us to say several particular things. For example, the definition points out that conflict is expressed with words or through nonverbal behaviors, such as tone of voice or facial gestures.

---

*When seen as communication, conflict is "expressed," as opposed to being "feelings" that happen inside a person.*

---

Stewart's definition concentrates on communication, not on psychology. It doesn't depend on speculating about or interpreting the motives of another person. In addition, the definition emphasizes that conflict is a natural part of human organizations. People have disagreements because they are different. Conflict is essentially about different points of views. Because we have not learned exactly alike, and because we see and value things differently, we vary in our beliefs as to what things are or should be.

---

*If we really want to "resolve" or eliminate conflict, we would have to eliminate our differences—or other people.*

---

(Maybe that's why the French philosopher Jean-Paul Sartre said, "Hell is other people." He might have understood the fundamentally social nature of our conflicts.)

It now makes sense why many managers and chief executives look upon conflict as a negative experience. It diverts their time and energy away from tasks. It represents the various issues that polarize individuals and groups within organizations. And it obstructs cooperative action and decreases productivity.

But this negative approach to conflict is the key to the problem. We need to begin seeing conflict as a creative and positive occurrence, also. Otherwise, we see the destructive implications of conflict carried too far for too long. We need to recognize that, as communication, conflict has some benefits.

## ◆ THE BENEFITS OF ORGANIZATIONAL CONFLICT

If conflict is inevitable and natural—if it represents the uniqueness of all people—then it is not always negative. If a major part of the problem about coping effectively with organizational conflict is our tendency only to think about the negative part of it, then we need to "mutate our metaphors" about conflict (see Chapter 3). We need to begin seeing the benefits of conflict.

The list of positive and creative values inherent in organizational conflict is equally long. Conflict has the potential to:

- Open up hidden issues

- Clarify issues

- Improve the quality of problem-solving

- Increase involvement in decision-making

- Increase cooperation and productivity

Conflicts can be valuable and productive, both for organizations and employees. For the organization, conflict can stimulate creative problem-solving, generate more effective ideas, and fine-tune working relationships. For employees, conflict can provide opportunities to test, expand, and demonstrate skills, better understand their organizations and co-workers, and develop confidence and trust. Specifically, organizational conflicts can help to:

1. *Develop more effective working relationships.* There is an energy potential that a legitimate disagreement can bring to our work relationships. It helps us learn something new about each other. We learn who we are. For example, there is a heated debate in a department about where a new computer should be located. Two employees want it in two different places, and the manager is caught in between. The manager could avoid the potential benefit of conflict by making an "executive decision" and ordering the computer to be put in one place or the other. Instead, he suggests a meeting bringing the main participants together. In the meeting, they develop an alternative solution. The three of them are able to locate enough funds to purchase a portable cart for the computer. They also work out a schedule for when the computer will be at a particular location. One result of the conflict is about tasks: A workable decision is made. But a second result is even more important: The two employees realize that they didn't handle the relational part of the conflict very well—they didn't initially sit down and talk. The conflict teaches them that they can talk with one another and they vow to "talk first, ask questions later" next time. They develop a more effective working relationship.

2. *Discover the "best" decision in a work situation.* The "adversary system" of our courts operates on the assumption that truth and justice usually emerge from the clash of ideas. The above example also shows how the clash of ideas and disagreements can lead to more workable organizational decisions. The manager was able to get the two employees to "own" the alternative decision because they both got to have their say.

   If the manager's decision to place the computer in one place or another had been imposed, one of the employees would have felt "disenfranchised."

He or she probably would have carried around some resentments about the decision that could have interfered with future performance, cooperation, and decisions. The decision was not necessarily the "best" decision they could have arrived at, but it was *productive*. It got the task completed and it maintained relationships. In addition, the employees felt a part of the decision and are more likely to respect it.

3. *Provide organizations a way to get feelings out in the open.* Here we must emphasize that we are not talking about allowing employees to scream at the wall or pound on a desk. Feelings must be communicated productively, too. We are talking about opportunities to explain feelings. Conflicts, if communicated through effectively, can be positive opportunities for getting feelings out; then they can be dealt with. As the example above also shows, if the energy of a feeling like anger can be channeled into a positive communication framework, the feelings can be used to find creative solutions and more workable relationships.

4. *Promote confidence in working relationships.* There is always uncertainty about what another person will do when things really get difficult. The first serious argument with any person is a major event, but the confidence that follows it can be even more important. Both employees in the above example can feel a new sureness, a new security. It is often those working relationships that avoid conflict that are fundamentally the most insecure and unproductive—they remain untested. Effective working relationships are tested by conflict, and trust and confidence develops by communicating successfully through those conflicts.

A positive attitude is the first step to effectively communicating through conflict. Managers and employees need to begin seeing conflict as creative and productive. The second step is to recognize that conflict comes in several types.

## ♦ TYPES OF ORGANIZATIONAL CONFLICT

Conflict is a pervasive part of all human experience, especially organizations. In fact, some philosophers have suggested that it is what makes us human. All humans are different and conflict is just a reflection of that natural condition. To eliminate conflict would mean eliminating differences; without differences, we would not be human.

But in order to communicate effectively through organizational conflict, managers and employees also need to recognize that not all disagreement is the same. There are three basic types of organizational conflict:

1. *There is conflict over organizational facts or interpretations.* This kind of disagreement reflects differing views over the *content* of objects or events.

They are disagreements over fact or meaning. We can disagree with the fact that Columbus landed in the Western Hemisphere in 1492 (which we can easily confirm or disconfirm) or we can disagree over whether he "discovered" America at all (which is a matter of meaning and interpretation). The most important question to ask yourself when dealing with this type of conflict is: What kind of content are you disagreeing about—fact or meaning? It makes a difference. Your labor contract may say that you are entitled to an office, but what does "office" mean? Is an office a separate work space or a single room divided into sections?

2. *There is conflict over organizational roles and identities.* This kind of disagreement reflects differing views over the *organizational roles* of people. As our first organization, you can see such conflicts in the family system. For example, Ken and his wife Liz are relatively new parents. They get to look forward to the time when their sons Nathan and Jamie come to think of themselves as "adults," but they continue to see them as their "little boys." (The role of an adult is quite different than the role of a child.) There will most assuredly be lots of conflicts. But the real question is: What will the conflicts be about? If Ken and Liz misinterpret the fundamental disagreement as conflict over facts, they may spend a lot of time arguing over details like who takes out the garbage or what time should they be home. On the other hand, if they recognize that the disagreements are about organizational roles—who defines who the boys are—then they can talk about identities and maybe work something out. They could consciously recognize that Nathan and Jamie are no longer "little boys," but are also not "full" adults. They could compromise with an intermediate role—increased, but limited, responsibilities and freedoms.

Now you may also see why *social labels* become so important to people and are often a source of conflict. Whether it be "gay," "African-American," "Hispanic," "Asian," "person," or "Native American," social labels proclaim conflict over fundamental issues of identity. Social labels are responses to real questions with real consequences: Who has the information, who has the authority, and who has the power to define people?

Regarding organizations, many conflicts about roles and identities focus on whether a person is considered informed or uninformed. As a manager, labeling yourself as informed is an important step in defining your position. In addition, organizational roles often center on who has what kind of authority in a given situation. On the job, an employee may agree that a manager has the authority to determine working hours, but not to be the custodian of clothing. Finally, conflicts in power relationships can also be understood as struggles over organizational identities and roles.

3. *There is conflict over organizational values.* Management researchers and managers have long recognized that organizations are social environments

as well as places where people earn money. Over a time period, most organizations develop a *culture* that strongly affects the way people view their place of work, its management, and its primary purposes. Although culture in organizations is defined as the common values of both managers and employees, cultural values are not imposed. They are developed over time. There can be disagreements over organizational values, such as over the level of expectations of all members of the staff, and regarding what service to customers means. In fact, conflict over cultural values may be necessary. Communication and human relations in organizations with well-defined, positive cultural values are nearly always better than in those that pay little attention to the values of the organization. There is value in communicating through conflict about organizational values, but they are most effectively dealt with in a structured way where there is an opportunity for mutual respect, learning, and maintaining interpersonal relationships.

Finally, the main point is to *identify the conflict*. If a conflict is over facts, identity, or organizational values, it must be communicated as such. Consequently, there is an advantage to knowing the type or "subject" of your conflict. But, whatever the subject, the final step in communicating through conflict is knowing what to do.

##  HOW NOT TO COMMUNICATE THROUGH ORGANIZATIONAL CONFLICT

The most important thing to keep in mind as you read this section is the difference between *reacting* and *responding*. We associate reactive behavior with the concept of "movement" we introduced in Chapter 3. Like movement, reacting is reflexive in nature. On the other hand, we consider responsive behavior more like the concept of "action." That is, responding is reflective. Responses "reflect" thinking and choices. Unlike reptiles who react, humans are "response-able"— able to respond.

The following ways of communicating through organizational conflict can be identified as reactive. A reactive approach does not see that whenever any employees disagree, there are always four elements to the communication: 1) You, 2) the co-worker, 3) the subject, and 4) the particular climate or situation. Figure 12.1 illustrates a circle where each one of the communication elements makes up one quarter of the circle. In order for the circle to be whole, it must include every element.

The first three communication elements of conflict are easy to understand. The *you* of a conflict is all of us as we deal with the second part of conflict—*other* people. The *subject,* of course, is what we are talking about. On the other

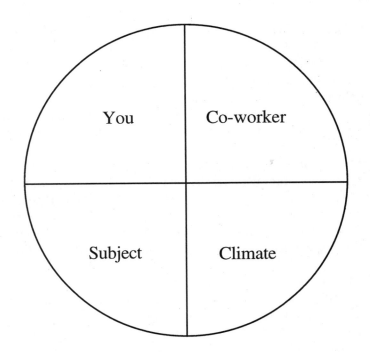

| | |
|---|---|
| You | Co-worker |
| Subject | Climate |

**FIGURE 12.1  THE FOUR ELEMENTS OF ORGANIZATIONAL CONFLICT**

hand, the last element needs further explanation. The *climate* of a conflict can be the physical environment and objects (on the phone, face-to-face; in the kitchen, office, or bedroom; the temperature of the room) but mostly it is emotional (past events, "baggage," emotional content of the subject).

If we "react," we communicate through conflict by ignoring or canceling out one or more of the communication elements. By reviewing the four communication elements of a conflict, we can identify four "reactive" or ineffective ways of communicating through conflict.

Virginia Satir defines the reactive styles in these four ways:

1. *"Placating" is when we ignore the "you" in conflict.* It is sort of a "better to keep the peace than to fight attitude" or "our relationship can't stand a fight." One example is when the other person in a conflict asks you, "What's wrong with my work? You respond, "It's not important." What you're saying is, "I'm not important." That's placating!

   Placating is an example of denying that a conflict exists. It is unresponsive because it fails to acknowledge the conflict. It avoids the conflict by using statements that terminate talking about the conflict before the discussion has thoroughly developed. It talks in generalities and avoids specifics, and is too relationally-oriented in its communication concerns.

When a person placates a conflict, he or she doesn't directly express his or her own feelings, thoughts, and wishes. Such people often communicate indirectly by frowning, crying, or whispering something under their breath. Or they may smile a lot, but they always subordinate their needs to those of others. You can picture the nonverbal behaviors—backing up, looking down, and other subordinate postures.

2. *"Pouncing" is when we try to ignore or eliminate the "other" employee in the conflict.* We pounce or blame a co-worker as a way of driving them away from the disagreement—we want them to placate. Pouncing is often based on the belief that "my view is the only right one" and on a dog-eat-dog assumption. Some signs of pouncing are name calling, rejection, hostile questioning, hostile joking, accusations, avoiding responsibility, and threats that demand a specified change in the other person's behavior.

   One example is when a co-worker in a conflict asks, "What's wrong my work?" The pouncer responds, "You're not capable of good work." What the pouncer means is, "You are not important." That's pouncing!

   Pouncing is an example of controlling a conflict. It is unresponsive because it fails to acknowledge the other person's opinions. When someone pounces, he or she tends to move with an air of superiority and intimidation. These people can run the gamut from "deadly quiet" to sarcastic and loud. Often they point fingers or make a fist. Pouncers are so intent on being right that they don't really hear what other co-workers are saying, even when you ask them a direct question.

3. *"Distracting" is when we try to change the "subject."* This assumes that if you change the subject, the conflict will go away. It doesn't. The clearest sign of distracting is an abrupt change of the topic. One example is when the other person in a conflict says, "We need to talk about our disagreements in the meeting today," and the distractor responds, "Did you see what Ralph was wearing today?" What the distractor means is, "The subject of the conflict is not important; let's keep things light and move on." That's distracting!

   Distracting is an example of diverting a conflict. It is unresponsive because it fails to acknowledge the subject of the conflict.

4. *"Computing" is when we try to ignore the emotional climate of conflict situations.* One example is, "Mature people don't get emotional." We now know that "feelings" always accompany "thought." The challenge in a conflict situation is to deal with emotion rather than ignore it. If you try to ignore it, that's computing! Computing is an example of dehumanizing a conflict. It is unresponsive because it fails to acknowledge the other person's feelings. When someone computes, he or she tends to remain impersonal. Such people use long and technical language. Often they only want to deal with "the cold, hard facts." "Computers" are so intent on being

detached that they talk in the third-person and remain expressionless as long as possible.

# ◆ CONCLUSION—RESPONDING EFFECTIVELY TO ORGANIZATIONAL CONFLICT

We identify the most effective way to communicate through conflict as *responding*. Responding is different from reacting. Responding implies thoughtfulness and an appreciation of relational communication. It responds to all four parts of the conflict—you, the other employee, the subject, and the emotional climate. It responds to feelings and "stands up for its own rights." It responds to the co-worker by asking about and listening for the other person's feelings and attitudes. Finally, it responds to the emotional climate of the conflict by learning to be comfortable with feelings, and to the specific subject by "sticking to the topic."

We conclude this chapter with some suggestions offered by Alan Sillars. Responding can be practiced by using certain kinds of relational and supportive statements (see Chapters 3 and 18). According to Sillars, "responding" to conflict involves:

- *Using descriptive language*—non-evaluative statements about observable events and behaviors related to the conflict.

- *Setting limits*—statements that explicitly qualify the nature and extent of the conflict (don't turn a content conflict into an identity conflict unless it already is one).

- *Being disclosive*—non-evaluative statements about "mental" events related to the conflict that the other person cannot observe, such as thoughts, feelings, intentions, motivations, and history.

- *Asking for genuine disclosure*—soliciting information from the partner about "mental" events related to the conflict that one cannot observe, and even soliciting complaints about oneself.

- *Offering support*—statements that express understanding, acceptance, or positive regard for the other person.

- *Emphasizing commonalities*—statements that comment on common ground.

- *Accepting responsibilities*—statements that attribute responsibility for conflicts to oneself or to both parties.

- *Initiating problem-solving*—statements that initiate mutual consideration of solutions.

- *Using relationship reminders*—reminding each other that the conflict exists within a broader context of mutual commitment and respect.

- *Reversing roles*—taking a couple minutes to each act out the other person's point of view.

- *Fractionating*—breaking conflicts down from one big mass into several smaller pieces.

- *Avoiding "triggers"*—triggers are less important but often initiate conflicts. They are the "last straw" but often treated like the "first straw." Again, learn to ask yourself, "Is this a conflict over content, identity, or values?" It makes a big difference.

- *Avoiding gunnysacking*—when a person refuses to use a conflict as an opportunity to bring up all the bruises he or she has been nursing for days, weeks, or even years.

- *Defusing*—asking yourself, "How well am I communicating through this conflict?" Defuse the conflict by listening, identifying areas of agreement, and maintaining your nonverbal cadence (don't do the "double-bind" as mentioned in Chapters 3 and 18). It might include moving to a better location without an "audience" or with less distractions or waiting until you have the time to really talk about the conflict.

---

*But remember, most of all, you can communicate most effectively through conflict by staying interpersonal.*

---

# ◆PART FOUR

## COMMUNICATING THROUGH ORGANIZATIONAL CHANGE

For the most part, the managing of organizational affairs is undertaken in small and large organizations alike without any special training in the skills required to cope with change. Often, the very communication and human relation behaviors of those trying to achieve change erect impenetrable barriers between managers and employees.

A major reason for the lack of more effective approaches to organizational change is the lack of the ability to communicate effectively through the processes of change that are rapidly taking place in today's organizations.

---

*Today, we do indeed need to communicate effectively*
*in a world of rapid organizational change.*

---

Change brings with it challenges for both employees and managers. Coping with organizational change mainly involves the appropriate understanding and use of communication and human relations skills. An organization can be described as the way people arrange their working relationships and get things accomplished through their communication. Success in accomplishing improved productivity, greater efficiency, or better service depends on how organizational members communicate through change.

The purpose of this part of the book is to introduce you to the issue of organizational communication and change. Change may be studied in a variety of approaches and dimensions. Part Four considers the communication aspect of change, especially how communication can help the manager respond effectively to common employee reactions to change.

## ◆ COMMON REACTIONS TO CHANGE

According to change expert Gordon Lippitt, employees and managers respond to many organizational changes, especially unplanned and poorly planned changes, in certain stages:

- *Shock*—an intense feeling of disequilibrium.

- *Disbelief*—a feeling of unreality about "why" the change is occurring.

- *Guilt*—a feeling that personal error has brought about the change.

- *Projection*—the act of blaming someone else for the change.

- *Rationalization*—trying to make sense of the change.

- *Integration*—attempting to turn the change into something positive.

- *Acceptance*—either through resignation or enthusiasm, the new state of affairs is accepted.

In general terms, such reactions are understandable when we consider how changes imply uncertainty about our future role in the organization and our future behavior in that role. Changes also imply uncertainty about who will be doing what, what we can expect from others, and what working relations we will have with others.

---

*Organizational ambiguity is unsettling; it generates a need to give meaning to change and understand it; it encourages a tendency to react in terms of the assigned meaning, whether correct or not.*

---

From the perspective of this book, the most effective way for employees and managers to understand and thoughtfully anticipate a change is to communicate. Information alone is seldom satisfactory. Information is always likely to contradict prior preferences or decisions. The contradiction between existing and new ideas creates a *state of dissonance,* which also must be dealt with.

Dissonance about change is most effectively reduced through attitudes—attributing favorable qualities to the change that are not obvious and attributing less favorable qualities to earlier held ideas. Consequently, the most effective way to communicate through change with co-workers is to recognize that communication needs to address both information (commands) and attitudinal (relations) needs.

---

*Communicating effectively through organizational change means recognizing employee command-oriented needs for accurate information, and employee relational-oriented needs for trust and security.*

---

## ◆ GUIDELINES FOR EFFECTIVELY COMMUNICATING THROUGH CHANGE

Managers who are responsible for helping employees through change have a variety of communication practices available to them. Of course, there is always forced compliance if the negative attitudes of employees are not important and new skills will not be needed by those who must make the change. Changing or replacing key people can be a strong force for change.

But if the goal is to communicate in a way that helps employees get accurate information *and* increase feelings of trust and security, a few guidelines for communicating effectively through change are suggested:

- *Include employees in discussions about change.* Resistance to change will be less intense when those who are affected, or those who believe they might be affected, know why the change is being made and what the advantages are. This can be done most effectively by letting them participate in the actual discussions about change, including planning sessions. Besides helping employees to understand the when, what, where, and why of change, discussions ease fears that management is hiding something from them.

In addition, open communication can stimulate many good ideas from those who probably are best acquainted with the problem that requires the change. It also alerts managers to potential problems that might arise when the change is implemented. Such an approach also involves employees in the diagnostic and creative processes.

- *Communicate accurate and complete information.* When employees are kept in the dark or get incomplete information, rumors start to circulate. This creates a communication climate of mistrust. Organizational rumors have an enormous influence on the productivity of employees and the general progress of change. Managers need to keep the official channels of communication open and try to eliminate rumors. If rumors continue to exist, employees can become increasingly more insecure about their status and future.

In addition, even when news is bad, employees would rather get it straight than receive no news at all. A lack of information makes employees feel helpless, while the whole story lets them know where they stand.

- *Give employees a chance to communicate their feelings.* Change is more easily assimilated when managers provide employees opportunities to communicate their feelings—to blow off steam. A gripe session can also give managers useful feedback about unsuspected reasons for opposition. For example, an employee may balk at using another copy machine because it is away from a window.

- *Communicate within the constraints of group norms and habits.* Managers need to know if a contemplated change will break up congenial work teams, disrupt commuting schedules, split up lunch partners, affect vacations, increase interpersonal conflicts, or violate a group norm.

- *Communicate adequate motivation.* Motivation affects a person's willingness to accept change. Resistance can be reduced if a manager communicates a meaningful reward. It varies with individuals. Employees may be concerned with self-expression, recognition, the need to feel useful and important, the desire for new knowledge, the need to meet new people, or a genuine desire to meet unmet needs.

- *Develop an overall trusting communication climate.* Mistrust about change arises when employees have inadequate information, when they are kept in the dark, and when rumors disseminate false alarms. One major reason for this is that they feel helpless—they cannot influence the process. To build a trusting communication climate, tell the truth. Given the facts, employees feel they are able to do something about a problem.

- *Make sure your communication also solves real problems.* One goal of your communication should be to identify the real problem. In improving group problem-solving, a number of challenges confronts the manager: a common perception of the problem situation, achieving an accepted value system by which the various alternative solutions can be judged, efforts by the group to influence each other, and achieving the final decision out of the choice of alternative solutions to the problem at hand. Of course, this is all in the context of dealing with tensions that arise in the group as a result of its problem-solving task activities.

---

*Managers who are responsible for helping employees through change and problem-solving activities must also help employees preserve social cohesion.*

---

## ◆ THE PURPOSE OF PART FOUR OF THIS BOOK

The purpose of the chapters in Part Four of this book is *to help you increase competence in communicating through organizational change by suggesting ways to deal with a variety of change situations.*

Chapter 13 offers attitudes that are the basis of effective communication in a new job situation. Chapter 14 discusses some human relations ideas that will help you communicate with culturally diversified co-workers.

Chapter 15 emphasizes the attitudes and skills needed to communicate effectively with new technology, such as e-mail. Chapter 16 concludes Part Four with a discussion regarding how to communicate constructive feedback. It argues that cooperation and productivity within an organization are greatly influenced by the quality of constructive feedback managers and employees receive.

# ◆CHAPTER 13

## COMMUNICATING IN A
## NEW JOB SITUATION

Undoubtedly you want to succeed on any new job or assignment you undertake. First, you want to prove to your family, friends, and management that you are a winner. Second, you want to prove it to yourself. There is a great deal at stake.

This chapter is devoted to ten tips that can help you in reaching your goal. If you take these tips seriously and apply them conscientiously, you can avoid many of the mistakes others make.

## ◆   TIP 1: BALANCE HOME AND CAREER

When you accept a new work challenge, it is vital that all home demands be under complete control. Your on-the-job concentration needs to be at a high level, and any home worries, especially those connected with small children or other relatives, can be distracting to both you and your co-workers. Balancing home and career, so that you can be a winner in both areas, is never easy to accomplish and maintain. The time to start (or reorganize) is *before* you accept a new job or assignment. Once things are out of balance, it may be too late for you to reach your full job potential. Give your career a break and get things organized at home *first*.

When it is necessary to call in ill, make every effort to talk to your supervisor or another management person. If a co-worker tells your boss you won't be in, doubts may be raised and your supervisor could call you for verification. Also, it never hurts to bring in a doctor's note to document an extended absence.

## ◆   TIP 2: TAKE A CALENDAR NOTEBOOK
## TO WORK WITH YOU

An abundance of important information—rules, regulations, and procedures—will be thrown at you at the beginning of a new job. The first days are days of adjustment and excitement, so don't trust yourself to remember everything.

Rather, buy an inexpensive calendar notebook and use it to record some of the instructions and hard-to-remember information you get from your supervisor or fellow workers. Jot these down as they are given to you.

Do not hesitate to take notes when receiving a complex answer to a question involving considerable detail. The notebook itself (if not overused) will create a good impression. It will help show that you are organized, methodical in your approach to learning, and serious about your career. In the evening, use the notebook to review certain facts and procedures. You can also use it to record appointment, ideas, names, and so on.

## ◆ TIP 3: ASK QUESTIONS, BUT LEARN TO ASK THE RIGHT ONES

Fear of being considered inadequate is the reason most people in a new work situation do not ask more questions. This is understandable, but it is better to ask questions than to suffer the serious results of continued mistakes. If you don't understand something, ask questions until you do. This may be necessary because those responsible for your adjustment and training do not always take enough time to explain things fully. Old hands tend to forget that they, too, had trouble learning at the beginning. They often talk so fast that only a genius or a psychic could get the message the first time around.

There is a right time and a wrong time to ask a question. One should not, for example, interrupt a person who is concentrating on getting a job done or who is communicating with others. There are also right and wrong questions. A right question is one you need to ask to be effective; a wrong question is one that does not apply to the task being explained. One should not, for example, ask questions that are answered in the orientation literature you have been given to read on your own time.

In asking questions, keep in mind that you must listen to the answers with your eyes as well as your ears. Sure, you receive the auditory impressions with your ears. But you should also look at the person who is speaking. Most people, in fact, feel it is discourteous when someone they are talking to lets his or her eyes wander. You will understand this if you have ever seen someone look at his watch, shuffle papers, stare at the floor, or look out a window while you are talking to him. You will make a better impression on people if you form the habit of listening with your eyes as well as your ears. You also stand a better chance of receiving any hidden—but vital—meaning that may lie under the message.

**TIP 4: USE GOOD JUDGMENT IN WORKING EXTRA HOURS AND TAKING YOUR BREAKS**

Some employees with a new opportunity attempt to secure their jobs and attract management's attention by working more than the normal number of hours at the beginning. They arrive first in the morning and make a point of leaving last at the end of the day. They often skip their breaks. This attitude, if sincere, is to be admired.

However, overzealousness can get you into trouble on two counts. First, there are usually regulations governing hours to be worked. On certain jobs, unauthorized overtime work and failure to take breaks can involve you and your employer in labor difficulties. It is important, therefore, always to abide by the instructions given to you by management.

Second, your fellow employees may misinterpret your motives and make life more difficult for you and your supervisor. Working extra hours and eliminating breaks when an important deadline must be met and when you are asked to do it by your supervisor is one thing, working extra hours only to impress others is quite another.

---

*As a rule, it is better to make full use of the time you spend on the job, rather than to try to impress others with your willingness to work extra hours.*

---

Many employees, especially those who are closely monitored by management, feel they need to immerse themselves in work as soon as they enter the workplace. It is often better to circulate around and send out a few friendly signals before digging in. Some people call this "doing a figure 8."

 **TIP 5: DON'T FLAUNT YOUR EDUCATION OR PREVIOUS EXPERIENCE**

You may have had more formal education than many of the people you will work with on your new job. But these people probably have far more on-the-job experience and practical knowledge than you do. That being the case, you would be wise to let them discover your educational background and experience gradually.

The job you are assigned may be more difficult than you expect. If you try to impress people with your experience or intelligence, they may not want to give you any help when you most need it.

If you are an experienced employee, you may have received your job training in another company. You will probably find that things are done differently in your new firm. Perhaps your way of doing things is better. But until you are sure, be safe and do it the way people at your new job do it. Give your co-workers the satisfaction of explaining how they do things. You will have plenty of time later to make changes that will be an improvement.

It is also a good idea to keep your salary to yourself. It is possible that another employee, doing work similar to yours as you start out, has yet to reach your salary level. Misinterpretation and resentment might occur. If so, both you and the other employee could lose.

## ♦ TIP 6: MAKE FRIENDS, BUT DON'T MAKE CLOSE FRIENDS TOO SOON

There are many little human-relations traps you can easily fall into in a new work environment. One of these is building one or two very strong friendships at the expense of all others. For example, suppose you discover that one of the employees in your department is extremely friendly the first day. Such friendliness is usually more than welcome the first few hours in a strange setting.

But beware. What if you spend all your time with this one employee and neglect being friendly to the others? What if this friendly person is not respected by the others? What if he or she has earned a poor reputation in the department and is offering you friendship from purely selfish motives?

Sometimes people who have failed to earn respect from others at work try desperately to win the friendship of a new employee. Remember that it is only natural that the other employees (including management) will quickly identify you with any employee or employees with whom you spend excessive time.

If one employee clings to you as you start your new job, you obviously have a difficult situation to handle. Of course, you should not be rude to this person. You will do well, however, to back away and be somewhat reserved toward this individual for the first few weeks and concentrate on building relationships with everyone.

## ♦ TIP 7: LOOK ENERGETIC, BUT DON'T BE AN EAGER BEAVER

Some people start their careers with a great burst of energy and enthusiasm that cannot possibly be sustained. These people frequently create a favorable impression to begin with, but later on are reclassified by both management and their fellow workers.

It is easy to be overeager at the beginning. You are new to your job, so you have a fresh and dynamic approach. You have a great deal of nervous energy to release. You are interested, and your interest motivates you to achieve. This desire to succeed, however, might cause you to reach too far too fast.

The best way to make progress inside an organization is to make steady progress.

Goal setting is a good idea and may help you achieve an even work tempo. Daily goals, written down and accomplished according to a priority system, make you a more productive and valuable member of the team. The practice will also help you in preparing for a supervisory role.

## ◆  TIP 8: DIFFERENT ORGANIZATIONS HAVE DIFFERENT PERSONAL-APPEARANCE AND GROOMING STANDARDS

A few organizations, such as factories, have no personal-appearance or grooming standards. They are interested primarily in your work performance and your human-relations ability.

Other companies, especially those that deal directly with customers, set minimum standards that are usually easy to live up to. Still other companies, like department stores, have rather high personal and grooming standards that may be difficult for some people to accept.

When you join an organization, you should carefully assess it and decide what is best for you and your future. You have a right to be yourself and protect your individuality. In doing so, however, you should weigh all factors and take into consideration that most people, including management, feel that a little conformity won't hurt you. You are responsible for meeting minimum dress standards. Managers quickly tire of those who try to slip by with unacceptable attire. They often interpret such behavior as immature.

## ◆  TIP 9: READ YOUR EMPLOYEE HANDBOOK AND OTHER MATERIALS CAREFULLY

Many organizations publish handbooks and other materials for their employees. These pamphlets usually contain vital information. Yet many employees, especially those with experience elsewhere, never read them.

Don't be casual in your use of company literature. Where else can you learn company policies that can keep you out of trouble? Where else can you discover important data that will prevent you from asking unnecessary questions? Take home all of the literature you are given and devote some time to it. Understanding your company and the benefits provided will not only help you start on the right foot, it will further your career.

# ◆ TIP 10: SEND OUT POSITIVE VERBAL AND NONVERBAL SIGNALS

There are many verbal signals you can use to create a good first impression—"good morning" and "thank you" are examples. Such easy signals of friendship should be transmitted at every opportunity to acknowledge the presence of others and to recognize any courtesies they have extended to you, however small.

A friendly person—one who creates a good first impression—is also one who uses nonverbal signals. For example, a person with a ready smile is easily interpreted as a friendly person. The smile seems to break any psychological barriers that might exist in a meeting of strangers. You immediately feel adopted by this person. A smile, then, is a friendly, nonverbal signal.

There are many effective nonverbal signals in addition to the smile. Shaking hands, gesturing positively with the hand or head, opening doors for people—these are all signals you send that make it easier for people to meet and know you. When you send out such signals naturally and in good taste, others do not feel awkward about approaching you. You have made it easy for them, and they like you for it.

In communicating a positive attitude to co-workers or clients, body language is most important. You probably have heard people say, "That's no problem," while their attitude (communicated through their body language) demonstrated that it was, indeed, a problem.

People who develop confidence in sending out such signals of friendship make excellent first impressions. They quickly increase their sphere of influence and build many lasting working and personal relationships. Have confidence in yourself and your ability to send out such signals. Take the initiative. Send out your own brand of signals in your own style and be a comfortable person to meet.

Remember, too, that the better you become at this, the better prepared you will be for any job interview you may face in the future.

# ◆CHAPTER 14

# COMMUNICATING WITH CULTURALLY DIVERSIFIED CO-WORKERS

The United States is a mosaic of many cultures—a culture being a group of people bonded together by ethnic backgrounds as well as values, attainments, beliefs, and traditions. A department or a corporation integrates employees into the workplace and, as a result, eventually develops a "culture" of its own.

What is your attitude toward cultural diversification? Will you be comfortable communicating with more and more co-workers from cultures other than your own? To give you an indication, complete the following scale.

---

## CULTURAL DIVERSIFICATION COMFORT ZONE SCALE

Place a check mark in the appropriate square and total your answers at the end of the scale.

|  | *Yes* | *No* |
|---|---|---|
| 1. Do you sometimes unknowingly favor co-workers from one culture over another? | ☐ | ☐ |
| 2. Do you find yourself spending more social time during breaks and lunch periods with co-workers from your own culture? | ☐ | ☐ |
| 3. Do you give full acceptance to new employees from one culture more slowly than those from another? | ☐ | ☐ |
| 4. Would you feel unmotivated and at a disadvantage if, for the first time, a new supervisor was from a different culture than your own? | ☐ | ☐ |
| 5. When working near co-workers from other cultures are you outwardly "cool" but inwardly resentful? | ☐ | ☐ |
| 6. Do you find that co-workers who have trouble with the English language irritate you? | ☐ | ☐ |
| 7. Are you less tolerant with co-workers who maintain aspects of their own cultures than those who fully adopt the American way? | ☐ | ☐ |
| 8. If you needed a co-worker to take your place while on a vacation, would you prefer to train someone from your own culture? | ☐ | ☐ |

*(continued)*

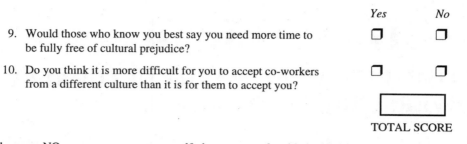

| | Yes | No |
|---|---|---|
| 9. Would those who know you best say you need more time to be fully free of cultural prejudice? | ☐ | ☐ |
| 10. Do you think it is more difficult for you to accept co-workers from a different culture than it is for them to accept you? | ☐ | ☐ |

☐

TOTAL SCORE

The more NO answers you gave yourself, the more comfortable it should be for you to work in the new culturally diverse workplace. However, you may wish to go back over the questions to see how many YES answers you could, with effort, move into the NO column. This may give you some idea of how easy or difficult it may be for you to work effectively with a more diverse cultural mix of workers in the future.

---

We have learned that it is not only what you produce yourself but how well you work with others that determines how much you contribute to your organization. What might you do to improve your attitude toward *all* co-workers regardless of cultural background? Here are three suggestions:

1. *As a permanent employee, take the initiative to build equally good relationships with all co-workers—especially those who are new and from a culture different than your own.* Go about this slowly. Translated, this means you should play the role of the friendly, helpful host, but not to the extent that you might put your relationships with your regular co-workers in jeopardy.

   Shirley is so friendly and outgoing that when a new employee arrives in her department she tries so hard to build a warm and friendly relationship that she makes it uncomfortable for the new arrival. Why is this? Because the new employee wants to win acceptance from *all* members of the team, and, if Shirley dominates her orientation, other employees may withdraw somewhat. You might even hear other employees say: "There goes Shirley again, trying to be a one-person welcoming committee."

   Try to be a comfortable co-worker to know, but do not move too fast. Give the new employee a chance to adjust slowly and build equally good relationships with all team members.

2. *Give those from different cultures the opportunity to demonstrate their special talents.* Nothing will make a new worker feel more comfortable than to win acceptance through their own performance. Their greatest need is to know that they can contribute. It is natural that newcomers in a work team or department feel shy or reluctant to express their special talents.

Sue Lin, raised and educated in Korea, arrived in the United States with unusually high computer and graphics skills. She decided, however, to soft-pedal them until she found a high degree of personal acceptance. Fortunately for Sue Lin, her team leader knew of her special abilities and brought them into play in a sensitive manner so that she was able to win acceptance based on her skills as well as her personal qualities.

Ramona Lopez is a graduate of the University of Mexico. When employed by her company, it was recognized that she had unusual artistic talent and would help the advertising department. In addition, she could communicate more effectively with customers from her culture, who were becoming a growing market for the product and services of the firm. However, this talent was not quickly recognized by Ramona's supervisor, who assigned her to dull work tasks. As a result, her co-workers underestimated the contribution she could make. Had it not been for Jeanne, who made a special effort to know Ramona and discover her background, Ramona might have become discouraged and left the company.

Obviously, when a new employee from a different culture becomes a member of a work team, adjustments must take place from both ends. In doing this, it is easy to underestimate the talents of the new employee.

The challenge of gaining acceptance may be more difficult for the new employee than we suspect. For example, let's assume that you work in a department where Caucasians, African-Americans, and Hispanics have already formed into a highly productive team. All three cultures have molded together into a single productive unit with little evidence of cultural conflict or disharmony. Then, for the first time, a Japanese individual is introduced as the new team member. While we, regardless of our cultural background, have already made the adjustment, the new Japanese person must, in effect, adjust to *three* different cultures. Our challenge is much easier than that of the newcomer.

3. *Apply the mutual reward theory.* Mutual reward means that both parties benefit from a relationship. The more equally the rewards balance out, the stronger and more permanent the relationship becomes. This theory performs best when each party is from a different culture, because they have more to learn from each other.

Jahal was educated in India and came to the United States to work for an export business—a firm eager to expand the market for their products in Jahal's native country. Initially, Jahal was very uncomfortable in the strange environment. After thirty days he felt at home and was willing to contribute ideas. Much of this was due to Grace, a co-worker in the marketing department, who tutored Jahal in American marketing concepts. When the marketing director decided to send Jahal on a promotional trip back to India, Grace was invited to go along; thus, Jahal had the opportunity to repay Grace for her training. As a result, both parties came out ahead, and the win-win philosophy of the mutual reward theory came strongly into play.

Nothing erases differences and prejudices faster than two people from different cultures who build a strong working relationship between themselves. Sooner or later the rewards balance out.

We do not always recognize our own prejudices toward those from different cultures. Sometimes, the only way to eliminate such prejudices is to get to know and understand each other by working closely over a lengthy period of time.

Fernando started working for the ACE Furniture Company after he graduated from high school. He gradually worked himself up from a warehouse worker to the rank of top delivery person. After two years driving and delivering, his assistant, also Mexican, resigned, and an African-American by the name of Hugo was assigned to him. Immediately, Fernando recalled the many fights between African-Americans and Mexicans in high school and figured he might have a challenge ahead of him. Hugo was also nervous about having a Mexican boss, wondering if he would receive fair and equitable treatment.

How did the relationship turn out?

For thirty days there was little communication, but slowly they came to know and understand each other's culture. Fernando talked a good deal about his family. Hugo talked about his interest in sports and why he was going to college at night. Eventually, a strong relationship developed. When Fernando was given a promotion to the head of the shipping department, he strongly recommended Hugo as his replacement. The fears based upon old high-school conflicts had dissipated, and a mutually rewarding relationship had been built.

Cultural attitudes are mental sets for or against those of a different culture. Often they are biases created from family values or information transmitted by the media. Many people have negative mindsets against another culture when they have never had the opportunity to work closely with a person from that culture.

For example, if an individual has been raised to stereotype all Mexican-Americans as weak in English skills, then what is needed is for that person to build a close relationship with a Mexican-American with excellent English skills; if an individual characterizes all African-Americans as unwilling to accept work responsibilities, then this individual needs to work closely with an African-American co-worker who works exceptionally hard and seeks responsibility.

Everyone in the United States faces the challenge of judging people fairly and on their individual performances regardless of cultural differences. Unless this happens, mutually rewarding relationships cannot exist. The best place to learn this vital human lesson is in the workplace. The more opportunities you have to work closely with those from other cultures, the greater your personal growth can be.

Since most prejudice comes from fear of the unknown, those who attempt to understand another person's way of life will be less prejudiced and less likely to stereotype.

Cultural diversity can strengthen departments and companies. Many culturally different people contributing diverse ideas can help departments find creative solutions to problems that a homogeneous team might not discover.

# ◆CHAPTER 15
## COMMUNICATING WITH NEW TECHNOLOGY

More than likely, you have recently been exposed to some new technology in the workplace. Computer-mediated technology and networking are changing the way people work and the way they communicate in organizations. Members of workteams use computer networks to communicate with each other and to access databases and programming tools. Workteams and employees communicate through electronic mail (e-mail), distribution lists, and bulletin boards.

Computer-based communication may even prove to be more significant than the personal computer revolution of a few years ago. Because the technology is used for communication, it affects the most critical process in an organization.

---

*The new technology of communication is about how people communicate; it is about the quality of organizational connections employees have with one another and with managers. It is about performance and success!*

---

We know that you want to succeed in the electronic workplace, and that you now appreciate how that means effective attitudes and communication skills.

This chapter is devoted to tips that can help you communicate effectively with the new technology of computers, specifically e-mail. Ours is a relational and organizational view of computer-based communication. We do not consider the technical details of how information technology (IT) works, but how the technology requires special ways of thinking, relating, and communicating. Our purpose is to help you to see how the changes of new technology can be capitalized on from a communication perspective. If you take these ideas to heart, you may be able to avoid many of the mistakes others have made in the electronic work environment.

We will start with some background information that relates the area of new technology to a general theme of this book: command and relational communication.

# ◆ ORGANIZATIONAL COMMUNICATION AND THE NEW TECHNOLOGY

If you want to stay current in the organization of the nineties and into the next century, you need to learn how to communicate effectively with computer technology. Futurists predict that information and access to it will be the basis for organizational communication in the next century. Whether you want to exchange information with your co-workers or join in a lively departmental meeting, the new technology will be your tool.

---

*Computer-based communication will bring employees and information together in a new dimension—an electronic, virtual organization where time, space, and communication have different meanings.*

---

E-mail, or online communication, is a good example. E-mail is electronic mail automatically passed through computer networks and/or via modems over common-carrier lines. (Actually, the word "e-mailed" means "embossed or arranged in a network" but has come to be shorthand for electronic mail.) E-mail is a popular application in organizations today. It is a very powerful organizational tool that is simple to use and easy to understand. It is hard to imagine any other form of computer-based communication that can be so intimate and yet so wide-reaching, so focused, and so expansive. An employee can communicate as easily with someone from another business across 12 time zones as with a co-worker in the same building.

Management researchers Lee Sproull and Sara Kiesler observe that the new technologies like e-mail are not just tools. Computer-based communication is extremely fast in comparison with interoffice mail, courier services, or postal mail. A message can be sent down the hall or halfway around the world in seconds. In addition, organizations appreciate the savings that result from reducing telephone tag and mail delays.

Sproull and Kiesler recognize the efficiency effects of a new technology like e-mail, but emphasize that such technologies have both efficiency effects and social effects. We have referred to this distinction as the difference between command and relational communication. Reducing communication costs is not always and automatically beneficial to organizational relationships. Faster and easier command communication is not always better relational communication. Because an electronic message is easier to send, employees may be tempted to "speak" before they think, and injured relationships may result (remember Chapter 10).

> *Changes we make to improve the efficiency of organizational communication have offsetting consequences for organizational relationships.*

Communicating with new technology is not simply a matter of adding hardware to an organization. Communicating with new technology leads to communicating and relating in new ways, and thereby to fundamental changes in how employees work and relate. In the following section, we outline some of the command *and* relational challenges of computer-based communication.

# ◆ THE CHALLENGES OF ONLINE COMMUNICATION

The challenge of communicating through e-mail or *online* is the inherent complexity of any human communication and interpretation. Even if the recipient of face-to-face communication fully understands what our words mean, misunderstanding can still occur because of faulty *attributions* (see Chapter 12). *What* (words) we communicate may be understandable; however, the *why* (attributions) may be fuzzy. But vague language involving lousy *referents* (what is symbolized by a word) also contributes to the formation of inaccurate attributions. Language itself can cause attributions to widely miss the mark.

Besides language, attributions are influenced by a wide variety of cultural, social, and contextual factors. In this regard, very clear attributions of other people's communication are often formed from just a small sample of messages. Essentially, the mind filters observations selectively, subject to recency and order effects. We then form a *prototype* (our initial metaphor) based on those observations and fill in the gaps of the prototype where necessary.

People are constantly involved in this type of "cognitive shorthand" as they strive to make sense of those around them. (While this dynamic is the basis of stereotyping, it isn't necessarily bad or wrong. We'd get extremely frustrated if it wasn't for this cognitive shorthand. It isn't necessary or even valid to try to stop the attribution process. Rather, the idea is to understand pitfalls and to avoid or reduce errors whenever possible.)

Organizational prototypes formed from attributions reflect organizational biases and information. A wide variety of biases have an important impact on organizational communication. It is inevitable that personal biases lead to prototype formation, attributions, and subsequent impressions. These impressions then influence subsequent communication in the organization. For example, we may communicate more warmly with a co-worker in the future if we attribute his or her behavior to being unlucky, as opposed to being lazy. We may be more respectful of a manager because we perceive him or her to be bright and lively.

*Faulty prototype formation, in valid attributions, and failure to understand communication through the eyes of other parties are all enhanced in online communication where information and feedback are restricted.*

E-mail communicators are particularly prone to faulty attributions because online communication excludes rich and significant cues on which people normally rely as information sources. As mentioned in Chapter 2, communication researchers have consistently found that nonverbal cues are the dominant source of meaning in interpersonal communication. One problem is that electronic conversations are missing body language and voice intonations, crucial elements of effective communication. When we take these elements away, people are forced to "fill in the blanks."

*Verbal communication (without voice inflection or tonality) is all we have with online communication.*

The challenge of communicating with a relative lack of information and immediate feedback in the asynchronous environment of e-mail communication, and the insidious nature of the prototype-building process that is part of attribution formation, quickly leads to anxiety and hostility. Online communicators can "fill in the blanks" with faulty attributions, establish incorrect prototypes, and blow things entirely out of proportion. Online communicators can come out of "left field" with surprising and often insulting language. Onliners refer to this type of communication as *flaming*. (Flaming can be defined as electronic messages or retorts that express startlingly blunt, extreme, and impulsive language because the technology lacks tangible reminders of the audience.)

In this regard, we have all probably been surprised by a hostile, flaming response to what we thought was an innocuous online communication. Faulty attributions usually lie behind every flame. A writer receives a message open to interpretation, lacks the nonverbal and paralinguistic resources to help interpret the ideas appropriately, assigns faulty attributions to the message, and reacts with anger and name-calling. When this happens, everything can go downhill fast!

How do we reduce the likelihood of faulty attributions and flaming in online communication? As a general rule-of-thumb, faulty attributions and flaming mindsets can be reduced by improving the quantity (commands) and quality (relations) of communication. A general implication of this point is that online communicators should check out assumptions more frequently and ask a lot more questions than they normally do in day-to-day, interpersonal communication.

We conclude this section with an outline of other—not necessarily good, not necessarily bad (but definitely different)—aspects of e-mail communication of which you should be aware:

- *Individuals and groups communicating in a computer-mediated environment are relatively more uninhibited.* "Flaming" is only one outcome of this dynamic. Online individuals and group members are also more willing to disclose personally sensitive information about themselves relative to face-to-face interaction.

- *Status differences play a lesser role in an online environment.* The fact that a person is The Chief Executive or The Boss or Knows What They Are Talking About has a less inhibiting effect on interaction. As a consequence of the low level of social information, individuals lose their fear of social approbation. On the other hand, interaction in online groups tends to be more evenly distributed among group members.

- *Online consensus decision making takes significantly longer than when group members interact face-to-face.* It tends to be more difficult for online groups to reach agreement. One difference is that tendencies to be interactive and outspoken in electronic discussions sometimes lead to increased group conflict. Such divergence means that electronic groups have to exert more effort trying to reconcile contradictory opinions than in face-to-face work groups.

The next section will build on our discussion of the nature of communication, online and otherwise, to include techniques for improving the quality of online communication. We will cover techniques—borrowed from traditional training material and adapted for online—intended to improve information and understanding and to lessen faulty attributions among online communicators.

## ◆ THE *WRITE* WAY TO COMMUNICATE ONLINE

The purpose of this section is to move from a general understanding of principles to the application of ideas in the online environment. To begin with, acronyms are helpful to remember useful concepts. In thinking through what's important in online communication—given problems such as the absence of nonverbal cues, problems with incomplete prototypes, inaccurate attributions, and so forth—friend, teacher, and author Chad Lewis has come up with an acronym that covers the essential skills of online communication. He calls it the *WRITE Way* to communicate online.

The WRITE Way to communicate online involves communicating in a manner that is (W)arm, (R)esponsive, (I)nquisitive, (T)entative, and (E)mpathetic. Here's an explanation of each component of the WRITE Way:

## (W)armth

Words on a screen are two-dimensional. Reading these words in isolation of usual communication cues lends itself to "coolness" that can lead directly to overreaction and flaming. Essentially, the goal is to interact with people, not with computers. In addition, online communicators sometimes lose perspective—acting as though messages are going into the relative privacy of a text file saved to the user's hard drive rather than being downloaded and read by perhaps hundreds, even thousands, of people. These people, in turn, read two-dimensional words in isolation and react. Pretty soon it's . . . BOOM! . . . communication that leads to embarrassment, chagrin, guilt, shame, and anger—in short, a whole plethora of potentially counterproductive human emotions.

Increasing warmth of online communication doesn't mean to be "touchy feely"—to give people the electronic equivalent of sloppy hugs and kisses. Rather, increasing warmth means to decrease the psychic distance among communicators. Being warm online is a way of affirming relational communication—it is about communicating with people.

In short, words can be "cold." We need to find effective ways to warm them up when communicating online. Here are ways to increase electronic warmth:

1.  *Use the telephone when necessary.* A telephone call to clarify a point or to negotiate a particularly sensitive issue is indicated when text just doesn't cut it. Some onliners think electronic messages should suffice for all communication, but an occasional phone call can be useful. We see this in the common revelation experienced when phoning someone with whom we have been communicating online. Invariably, the confirmation that we are all human and not just words on a screen is the first thing discussed when voice connection is made.

2.  *Send sensitive information to private mailboxes.* It's usually much more helpful to offer "constructive feedback" (see Chapter 18) privately. This approach is akin to offering feedback behind closed doors.

3.  *Incorporate warmth into the written text.* Professional writers are able to convey a wide range of emotions. It is much tougher for normal mortals to do this. We have found it helpful to occasionally write about our families and interests. Sometimes we tell a bad joke (though the joke needs to be a "sure thing" because humor easily backfires online). Describing the setting from which you are writing, the weather or music to which you're listening, can help readers place you in a human setting.

Playing with language and its symbolism also adds warmth as long as it is not overdone. One way to play with language and symbols online is to use an occasional *emoticon* in your writing. Emoticons represent a way of bringing so-called "nonverbal" cues into online communication though, technically, they are not "nonverbal" communication in the usual sense of the word. As we mentioned in Chapter 2, authentic nonverbal communication is beyond our control. It is not necessarily a conscious effort to communicate a particular meaning and it is readily open to other people's interpretations.

Emoticons are conscious and intend the reader to accept a certain tone or meaning. Emoticons, because they are conscious symbols with intent, cannot be trusted like true nonverbal communication, but they do serve a purpose online. As part of a long-term relationship with established trust, they can warn readers not to misinterpret certain words. Table 15.1 lists some of the more common ones.

**TABLE 15.1  EMOTICONS AND THEIR MEANINGS**

| | | |
|---|---|---|
| 1. | :-) | **User smiling** |
| 2. | :-( | **User sad** |
| 3. | :-< | **User very sad** |
| 4. | :-\ | **User undecided** |
| 5. | :-p | **User sticking tongue out** |
| 6. | :-D | **User talks too much** |
| 7. | :-o | **User surprised** |
| 8. | :-O | **User shocked** |
| 9. | :-{ | **User has mustache** |
| 10. | :-\| | **User has no expression** |
| 11. | :-& | **User tongue-tied** |
| 12. | :-t | **User cross** |
| 13. | :-@ | **User screaming** |
| 14. | :-x | **User lips sealed** |
| 15. | :-e | **User disappointed** |
| 16. | ::-) | **User wears glasses** |
| 17. | ;-) | **User winking** |
| 18. | (-: | **User left-handed** |
| 19. | >:-< | **User mad** |
| 20. | \|-) | **User bored** |

## (R)esponsiveness

"Asynchronous communication" means people sometimes wait several days before getting a response to a message. Not only is there a lack of the usual communication cues, but there is also the need to wait for feedback. As noted previously, this waiting can feed into invalid attributions ("Ken hasn't replied! Hmmm . . . guess he doesn't really think much of my ideas"). A misinterpretation seems to be magnified by the passing of time and can be blown up into a major problem.

A solution is to:

1. *Set deadlines or otherwise be consistent in terms of when you give feedback.* This allays anxiety and creates an expectation on the part of others of when they should hear back from you. Once this expectation is satisfied through timely provision of feedback, trust will be reinforced (a positive contributor to warmth). Generally speaking, try to return messages as soon as possible. As we mentioned in Chapter 2, temporal relations or chronemics are a particularly important nonverbal for e-mail communication. Attitudes toward responsiveness are communicated by the ways individuals deal with time online. If they are late with their replies, they send a message of indifference to others.

2. *Remember to provide occasional reminders.* Another aspect of responsiveness is redundancy. Think of issuing reminders as a proactive type of responsiveness. An interesting aspect of online communication is that it is possible to have a perfect memory of what "was said." Unfortunately, it is difficult to access a recollection if it is buried in hundreds of kilobytes of information. Consequently, don't be surprised if people fail to act on an online request, particularly if information is part of a larger message or part of a succession of messages on related topics. The use of short messages and redundancy helps to allay this problem and keeps online communicators on track.

## (I)nquisitiveness

Defensiveness is reduced if people ask questions rather than make statements. It is usually more constructive to ask a person "why" than it is to tell them "what." Inquisitiveness serves two important purposes: Besides reducing defensiveness, it often provides information that is useful for solving a problem, resolving an issue, or whatever. Bringing valid information to bear on online communicative exchanges is almost always a good idea.

1. *Be sure to ask questions.* Online defensiveness tends to be reduced when people ask questions rather than make statements.

## (T)entativeness

Defensiveness is reduced when people hear or read, "It appears that . . ." as opposed to, "It is. . . ." Inquisitiveness and tentativeness work well together. A question—framed in a tentative manner—reduces defensiveness and can also contribute valuable information (e.g., "Don't you think it'd be better if we . . .).

1. *Use tentative language and posturing, unless the situation dictates otherwise.* The old concept of sending "I" rather than "you" messages works as well in online writing as it does in oral interaction. It is often better to say or to write "I believe . . ." rather than to say or write "you are. . . ."

Sometimes you must make absolute statements. You must occasionally send "you" messages. Communication would otherwise degenerate into a sloppy, gooey, indeterminate mess, not unlike conversations that occur when a bunch of egoists get together to talk out a problem. When to be absolute and when to be tentative is up to you. It is a judgment call.

## (E)mpathy

An important aspect of online communication is to:

1. *Put yourself in the shoes of your audience.* Always consider your online audience. There is a wide variety of issues to keep in mind. For example, a person can be a highly effective, intelligent contributor to an online group even if he or she misspells words or doesn't write well.

As noted previously, a wide range of cultural, contextual, and social issues affect the frame of reference people bring to online communication. Empathy also involves inquisitiveness. An idea we have always found to be helpful is to be inquisitive if you need information to better understand your audience. Ask a lot of questions if necessary. This need goes back to the inherent difficulty of invalid attributions and prototype formation in online communication.

To summarize this section, The WRITE Way to online communication involves communicating in a manner that is (W)arm, (R)esponsive, (I)nquisitive, (T)entative, and (E)mpathetic:

*(W)armth* means to:

- Use the telephone when necessary.

- Send sensitive information to private mailboxes.

- Incorporate warmth into text.

*(R)esponsiveness* means to:

- Set deadlines, or otherwise be consistent, in terms of when you give feedback.
- Remember to provide occasional reminders.

*(I)nquisitiveness means to:*

- Be sure to ask questions.

*(T)entativeness means to:*

- Use tentative language and posturing, unless the situation dictates otherwise.

*(E)mpathy means to:*

- Put yourself in the shoes of your audience.

 ## CONCLUSION—THE NETIQUETTE OF ONLINE COMMUNICATION

Is there such a thing as proper "netiquette"? Yes, and it is a good thing, too! It is easy enough to use e-mail but, as you have seen, there is an art to communicating effectively online. We conclude this chapter with a few additional tips for making friends and influencing people online, and for avoiding unnecessary conflicts, or what we call "flames":

- *Keep your messages brief and to the point (unless it is a work assignment where your supervisor or teacher asks for important details and examples).* If you want to make sure people listen to what you have to say, do not bore and confuse them with rambling messages that tend to be skipped in favor of shorter messages that concentrate on one subject. Stick to the subject of that particular discussion.

- *If you are responding to a message, quote the relevant and specific passage or summarize it for those who may have missed it.* Do not make people guess about what you are talking about, especially if you are responding to a particular message. Highlight the message that you are responding to right up front (often with a symbol like >) and then follow with your response. One example:

  > What time do you want to meet tomorrow?

  Mike—2:00 pm will be fine. See you there! Sue

- *Don't start a "flame war" unless you are willing to take the heat.* Just as you shouldn't drive when you are angry, you should not send e-mail responses when you are mad at someone. Go ahead and type a response, but do not mail it until the next day. Chances are that when you come back later to read your response, you'll be glad that you did not send it.

- *Never copy someone else's writing without permission or citation.* Acknowledge your sources. Define the difference between what others have written and what you think. State your own contribution.

- *Don't clutter discussions with short "I agree" and "Me too!" messages.* It is very frustrating to find lots of messages with very little substance. Remember that e-mail communication can be "labor-intensive" and that it takes time to read numerous messages.

- *Don't type in all caps. (IT'S LIKE SHOUTING!)* You can do it once in a while for strong emphasis, but only for individual words.

- *Don't flame people for bad grammar or spelling errors.* Spelling and correct grammar are important, but online communication tends to be informal. Even though sloppy messages that are full of errors stick out, the principle of constructive feedback that says effective feedback is solicited should be followed.

Now go ahead and enjoy your electronic journey!

# ◆ CHAPTER 16
## COMMUNICATING
## CONSTRUCTIVE FEEDBACK

As Chapter 1 emphasized, in order for organizational communication to be effective it must involve the production of adequate feedback. A lack of feedback significantly affects the quality of command communication, making oral instructions and written publications vague and open to misinterpretation.

In addition, Chapters 2 and 3 showed how organizational communication is also about relationships. Consequently, a lack of feedback significantly affects the quality of relational communication, making working relationships and superior–subordinate communication much more difficult.

---

*Communication problems with organizational feedback*
*processes interfere with interpretation*
*of information and relationships.*

---

This chapter argues that cooperation and productivity within an organization are greatly influenced by the quality of constructive feedback. We stress the idea that supportive communication is the basis of an open communication climate, promoting constructive feedback. In turn, constructive feedback is an integral part of an effective performance review system. We wish to help you understand why feedback problems sometimes develop and to show you how you can best provide supportive communication and constructive feedback to other organizational members.

## ◆ SUPPORTIVE AND DESTRUCTIVE COMMUNICATION

The basis of constructive feedback is *supportive communication*. In a now-famous essay, Jack Gibb described the characteristics of supportive communication and of its opposite, defensive-arousing communication, and thereby established the underlying principles of constructive feedback. Gibb concluded that communication creates feelings of discomfort and defensiveness when either its content or the way in which it is presented makes people feel that they are being:

- *Judged*
- *Manipulated* or controlled inappropriately
- *Tricked* into believing that they are having an effect on decisions when they are not
- Subjected to *cold, impersonal and uncaring treatment*
- Treated as a r*elatively useless person*
- *Preached to* by "know-it-all" managers

Gibb recognized that a supervisor's communication can either support or attack an employee's sense of worth and security. Just as we discussed in Chapter 2, Gibb saw that communication can be either "person-building" or confidence destroying.

---

*Supportive communication creates feelings
of personal worth and comfort.*

---

The difference between defense-arousing and supportive communication is *how* the messages are communicated. Sometimes neutral, or even positive, messages are communicated in such a way that the content becomes negative. For example, excessively strong or too public praise can lead to unnecessary defensiveness on the part of the employee. Defensiveness on the part of one, both, or all parties to a particular communication act puts up barriers to the achievement of worth and comfort. It is as though people literally put up walls or don suits of armor, making it difficult for feedback to get through.

After observing communication within groups for several years, Gibb identified six types of destructive communication (because it destroys self-esteem rather than builds it) and six types of contrasting supportive communication (because it builds persons and reduces defensiveness). Table 16.1 contrasts destructive and supportive communication.

### TABLE 16.1   GIBB'S CLASSIFICATIONS

| *Destructive Communication* | *Supportive Communication* |
| --- | --- |
| • Evaluative | • Descriptive |
| • Controlling | • Participatory |
| • Manipulative | • Genuine |
| • Impersonal | • Interpersonal |
| • Superior | • Equal |
| • Certain | • Tentative |

*Evaluative v. Descriptive.* What is the difference between saying to another that, "You're always late to work!" versus the statement, "I've noticed that you've been late the last two days"? Both statements pertain to the same behavior. The real difference lies in how the message is communicated.

It is more supportive to describe behavior to another than it is to evaluate that behavior in an absolute fashion. It is also more supportive to send "I messages" than "you messages." "I messages" are less likely to lead to defensive behavior because they describe a person's behavior (lateness) rather than the person himself (you!).

*Controlling v. Participatory.* People become defensive when another person attempts to control a solution or a future activity. "You'll do it because I told you so!" is probably the clearest example of this type of negative communication. Bases of control are many: A person may be the boss, a parent, a teacher, or simply someone who is louder and bigger than another party in a communication.

A contrasting, supportive approach is to let the other person participate in the defining and solving of a problem. The idea is for communicators to find common ground, to find a "win-win" solution to a problem.

*Manipulative v. Genuine.* The goal is to avoid communicating in a manipulative way. For example, if you only concentrate on the "command" function of communication, you run a better chance of being seen as manipulative. "Relational" communication is perceived as less fixated on the task and more open to the human issues of trust and emotion. On the other hand, if others *believe* you are being manipulative, "the wall" still goes up. Simply creating the appearance of sincerity can be seen as manipulative. Genuine relational communication says that the human factor is a necessary part of the whole communication process.

*Impersonal v. Interpersonal.* Remember the last time you interacted with a sterile, seemingly uncaring individual in an institutional setting? It may have been a clerk at a local state office, a physician, an Internal Revenue Service agent, or a professor. The studied neutrality of people in these settings raises our defenses. We may find ourselves relating to these people as though they are machines, rather than as unique, thinking, and feeling human beings.

In the workplace, managers are often guilty of indifference to the needs of subordinates. Sometimes managers believe such indifference is professional because of the situation. It is, however, quite possible to be interpersonal to employee concerns and still maintain professionalism.

It's not the situation that determines whether communication is supportive, but the quality of that communication.

Managers can be interpersonal, which involves looking at any situation from a relational perspective (see Chapter 3 and the Impersonal–Interpersonal Continuum), without compromising professionalism. Gibb found that interpersonal communication helps to remove the quality of indifference from communication and reduces defensiveness.

*Superior v. Equal.* Think back to a boss with whom you enjoyed working. This boss probably made you feel as though you and she were "on par." Arrogant people, on the other hand, may cause you to become defensive and go on the attack.

We all have limitations and weaknesses. No one has cornered the market on brains, talent, or general ability regardless of their position on an organizational chart. Truly supportive managers seem to realize this fact.

*Certain v. Tentative.* Don't be too sure you know the answer to a problem. Even if you are sure, listen to what others have to say. It is usually much more supportive to frame a problem or raise an issue in a tentative way. For example, statements such as "It appears as though . . . ," "Don't you think . . . ," or "I believe . . ." communicate tentativeness much better than statements like "I know that . . . ," "You're wrong . . . ," or "I'm right. . . ."

As mentioned in Chapter 3, when successfully and consistently used, supportive (relational) communication increases the level of trust between supervisors and subordinates and, generally, between co-workers. It creates the perception (and we hope the reality) that an organization is "employee-centered." In fact, as we will discuss in the next section, supportive communication is the foundation of an open communication climate in an organization.

# ◆ SUPPORTIVE COMMUNICATION AND OPEN COMMUNICATION CLIMATES

Although the concept of openness is difficult to define, it depends on employees' feelings that their supervisors encourage them to initiate communication on either personal or work-related topics. But it is clear that supportive communication is fundamental for creating an open communication climate in organizations.

---

*If managers attack or fail to acknowledge the worth
and competence of their employees, an open
communication climate cannot be established.*

---

Gibb's work suggests that an open communication climate is created when supervisors actively encourage their employees to communicate with them, and when they are careful to judge the content of communication and not the communicators themselves.

---

*Employees must feel that they will not be punished when they do
initiate difficult communication, even if the information reflects
negatively on themselves, their work, or their supervisor.*

---

The communication climate in which one works is an extremely important condition that cannot be overlooked. In climates where distrust is high and the need for politeness is uppermost, it is extremely difficult to practice genuine supportive communication. It is also the kind of climate in which supportive communication is most needed.

Unfortunately, the tendency for organizations to adopt the language of supportive communication without encouraging behavioral changes leads to employee distrust and decreased job satisfaction.

From the perspective of this book, the potential success for establishing an open communication climate in any organization depends on two key aspects: 1) using supportive communication to establish a general sense of mutual trust and respect, and 2) practicing the specific principles of constructive feedback.

Generally, organizations can begin the process of establishing open communication climates by encouraging managers to:

- Help individuals better understand the communication process.

- Give correct feedback to an employee about how others perceive his or her behavior.

- Help a person get better information as to the effects of his or her own behavior, so that, if desired, it can be modified.

- Help employees to see how they might be pre-judging or coloring their listening.

But unless individual managers learn specific practices that are appropriate, supportive communication can become merely a new and different way of manipulating people. The next section will concentrate on how individuals can initiate steps toward a more open communication climate in their organizations by learning how to practice constructive feedback.

## ◆   PRACTICING CONSTRUCTIVE FEEDBACK

It is not always easy to practice supportive communication. The cold and impersonal communication climates of many organizations often put the emphasis on "laying another person out cold." Such climates seldom lead to the warm support of relational communication behaviors or collaborative problem solving. Power often determines the goal to be venting one's own opinions, rather than helping a co-worker. Supportive communication is not always in keeping with a sole reliance on organizational commands.

But on a personal level, individuals can initiate the process by developing key attitudes and skills with respect to their own communication behaviors. One way is by fostering competence in *constructive feedback*. Constructive feedback uses supportive communication to relay precise information to an employee about what he or she did well (or not so well) in order to maintain a positive working relationship. It puts the ideas of supportive communication into practice.

---

*Constructive feedback builds trust and people!*

---

The first step is attitudes. You might think of the following as the necessary knowledge areas for developing competence in constructive feedback. Along with an understanding of the characteristics of supportive communication, these areas are the basis for practicing effective constructive feedback skills.

They include:

- An awareness that your feelings influence your communication.
- An appreciation of other people's feelings and how they affect their communication.
- The desire to build feelings of security in other people.
- The empathy to listen from another's point of view, rather than just from your own.

- The willingness to take more than half the responsibility for the success or failure of communication.

- The courage to accept constructive feedback in all your own activities.

- The openness to hear what the other person says and not just speculate and act on imagined motives.

- The acceptance that communication is imperfect.

The second step is practicing the skills. As you learned in Chapter 4, "communication competence" is about both knowledge and skills. Consequently, the above knowledge areas need to be followed through with actual communication behaviors and practices. By synthesizing Gibb's classifications, we offer some specific skills to practice when giving constructive feedback to another person:

1. *Focus on behavior rather than on the person.* It is important that we refer to what a employee does rather than to what we think he or she is. We might say that a person "talked more than anyone else in this meeting" rather than that he or she is "pushy." To be told that one is "dominating" will probably not be as useful as to be told that "in the conversation that just took place, you did not appear to be listening to what others were saying, and I felt forced to accept your arguments." The former approaches imply a fixed personality trait, the latter ones allow for the possibility of change.

   It is easier for employees to change behaviors than to change personalities. Describing one's reactions to behavior allows employees to judge the behavior for themselves and to decide how to use it or not use it. The goal is to focus on specific observations, not on inferences. By avoiding psychological language or speculating on motives, you reduce the need for the other individual to respond defensively. It encourages the other person to make sense of their own behavior.

   Focusing on behaviors also allows us to share information rather than give advice. By sharing information, we give the person responsibility for helping to decide if the feedback is appropriate and in accordance with important goals and needs. When we give advice, we take away important degrees of freedom and discourage taking responsibility. Sharing information puts the focus on developing alternatives, not merely on accepting solutions.

2. *Take the needs of the employee into account.* Feedback is destructive when it serves only our own needs and fails to consider the needs of the person on the receiving end. Constructive feedback is given to help, not because it makes us feel better or gives us a psychological advantage. It should also focus on the kind and amount of information the other person can assimilate and use.

3. *Direct your feedback toward behavior the employee can change.* Frustration and aggressive resistance are only increased when a person is reminded of shortcoming over which he or she has no control. *Attribution theory* tells us that the willingness to change depends on our ability to see our own efforts contribute to success. Success must be perceived to be caused, at least in a substantial part, by our own efforts. As teachers, we know that students who believe their efforts influence their achievement are more likely to learn than are students who believe that learning depends on teachers or something else beyond their own control. If a manager concentrates on a behavior that an employee has very little power to change, he or she is encouraging "learned helplessness" in that employee—a feeling that one cannot overcome failure.

4. *Help employees to "own" the feedback.* Constructive feedback is most useful when the employee is given the chance to formulate the kind of questions that improve performance. It should be given in the kind of communication climate that encourages the employee to actively seek feedback. For example, employees can be asked to identify some of the issues that will be the focus of one of their own upcoming performance reviews. They are then encouraged to be responsible for identifying their strengths and weaknesses in those areas and ways of enhancing and improving performance. One employee may concentrate on managing meetings more effectively while another may look at how to improve public presentations. Constructive feedback is more often solicited than imposed.

5. *Time your feedback.* Timing is important. The information should be current in time and space. Constructive feedback is most useful immediately after the observed behavior. The employee more readily understands how the information relates to his or her intentions, and thus is in a position more readily to accept alternative patterns of behavior for trying to solve problems. To the degree that there is a delay in the communication of significant information, there is forgetting, and often what is forgotten is a particular factor that would promote the necessary change in behavior.

   In addition, the reception and use of constructive feedback involves many possible emotional reactions (such as readiness), and excellent feedback given at the wrong time may do more harm than good.

6. *Check your feedback for clarity.* Having the employee paraphrase the feedback gives the supervisor an opportunity to check the accuracy of his or her feedback to an employee (see Chapter 1). If a manager uses terms that are vague or abstract, it is hard for the employee to understand. To communicate vague ideas leaves wide latitude for personal misinterpretations of the meaning the manager is attempting to convey and enhances the chance of defensive behavior on the part of the employee. "Consensual validation" is of value to both superior and subordinate.

7. *Consider your feedback as part of an ongoing working relationship.* Constructive feedback opens the way to a relationship with another person built on communication, growth, and concern. Through such relationships, everyone becomes senders and receivers of valuable feedback and experiences.

# ◆ CONSTRUCTIVE FEEDBACK AND THE 3 RS OF PERFORMANCE REVIEWS

The most common organizational practice in need of the knowledge and skills of constructive feedback is the performance review. A performance review occurs whenever a manager and a subordinate discuss performance appraisal results. As a way of summarizing this chapter, performance reviews reflect the principles of constructive feedback to the extent that they satisfy the three "Rs" of effective reviews: They are relevant, relational and reinforced. (See Figure 16.1.)

---

*Performance reviews are examples of effective constructive feedback when they are relevant.*

---

"Relevancy" is when 1) the feedback is specific to the employee's performance and 2) the feedback is timely to the employee's needs. Specific feedback involves relaying to the employee precisely what he or she did well (or not so well). Speaking in general terms, such as "Well, Michael, you did a good job on the Anderson account but you could have done better with the Higgins account," fails to tell Michael specifically how his performance could be improved. What is meant by "good" or "bad"?

Specific behavior or performance measures ("Michael, you completed executive summaries for all meetings with Mr. Anderson" or "Michael, you were late to all four meetings with Mr. Higgins") are much more relevant and more likely to help Michael improve his performance.

Relevant feedback should also be timely. Deviations from preferred behavior or performance should be corrected quickly so that the individual or group objectives can be reached. Feedback should be timed to respond to the relevant deviations. Productivity can be increased if deviations from standards are corrected in a timely manner.

---

*Performance reviews are examples of effective constructive feedback when they are relational.*

---

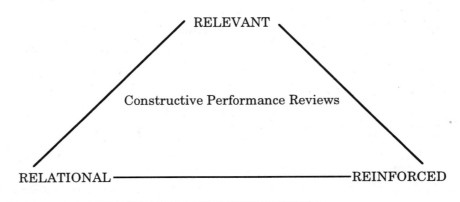

**FIGURE 16.1  THE THREE RS OF CONSTRUCTIVE
PERFORMANCE REVIEWS**

They are "relational" when they treat the employee interpersonally—as a unique, thinking, and feeling individual. It is clear that feedback based on general personality traits leads to employee dissatisfaction. It tends to offend a person's sense of uniqueness and offers no specific behaviors to change. But interpersonal is not necessarily about personality. It is mostly about the quality of communication.

Performance appraisal based on behavior and/or output can eliminate the problem of personality and still be interpersonal. The supervisor emphasizes that he or she is critiquing performance on the job *and* recognizes the unique characteristics the employee brings to the job at the same time. The supervisor allows the employee to think through alternative solutions to a problem and to choose the most appropriate response. The supervisor also responds to any feelings the employee might have about the process.

*Performance reviews are examples of effective
constructive feedback when they are reinforced.*

"Reinforcement" is when performance reviews are 1) acknowledged by the employee and 2) held frequently by the organization. Reinforcement is a dynamic relationship between the individual employee and organizational values. First, if feedback is to improve productivity, it must be ultimately acknowledged and "owned" by the employees themselves. Employees can be encouraged to suggest areas to review in their own performance. Self-assessments can be a part of the performance review process, including personal action plans—steps employees devise to correct deficiencies and build on past successes.

Second, organizations reinforce the value of performance reviews by holding them frequently. Frequent reviews contribute significantly to the success of the performance appraisal system. They tell employees that management is committed to performance appraisal and is not simply paying "lip service" to a management fad. They also provide for timely corrective action and contribute to higher employee satisfaction with supervisors.

But frequent feedback is *not* the same thing as close supervision or "micromanaging." Performance review sessions should be planned and should take place so that privacy is maintained.

 ## CONCLUSION—THE DUAL NATURE OF CONSTRUCTIVE FEEDBACK

Negative feedback actually reduces productivity. Too much criticism becomes unmanageable and disconfirming.

---

*Avoiding feedback is not the solution to the problem.*

---

Managers can constructively face the challenge that it may be difficult to review performance constructively. As we have discussed, employees are more receptive to feedback when they are evaluated in a timely manner about factors directly related to work performance (relevant), allowed to participate fully in the performance review process (relational), and if they see that performance plans and objectives are continually and frequently discussed in their organizations (reinforced).

In addition, managers should avoid the "double-bind" in feedback situations (see Chapter 3). The double-bind is a statement made at two communication levels in which the non-verbal context (or meta-message) of a message appears to invalidate that message. A double-bind is where the verbals and nonverbals of communication don't match. For example, having a so-called "objective" or "professional" facial gesture while giving very positive feedback is confusing to an employee and reduces the credibility of the supervisor and the information. Likewise, being too cheerful while giving seriously negative feedback does the same thing.

---

*In communicating constructive feedback to co-workers,*
*body language is as important as the information.*

---

Saying, "You're doing a great job," while your body language is demonstrating that that is not the case, is not supportive or constructive.

People who develop competence in giving constructive feedback are people who understand that effective communication has a dual nature of offering information and building a positive relationship. Constructive feedback is a balance between what we say and how we say it. Remember this and you'll grow more comfortable and competent at giving constructive feedback to others.

# ◆PART FIVE

## COMMUNICATION AND CAREER DEVELOPMENT

As this book has tried to emphasize throughout, the key to success in career development is the ability to adopt appropriate organizational communication attitudes and styles.

In 1972, organizational theorists Rod Hart and Don Burks introduced the concept of *rhetorical sensitivity*. They argued that leadership is enhanced, organizational communication is most effective, and working relationships are most stable and rewarding if managers are "rhetorically sensitive" and communicate in ways reflecting that sensitivity.

The purpose of this section of the book is to introduce you to the organizational theory of rhetorical sensitivity. One of the theory's strengths is that it provides a set of sensible principles that can be used by employees and managers to achieve more effective organizational communication and career advancement. We begin by comparing and contrasting the Rhetorical Sensitive communication style with two other types identified by Hart and Burks: Noble Selves and Rhetorical Reflectors.

## ◆ CAREER DEVELOPMENT AND COMMUNICATION STYLES

Individuals have a predominant manner or style in which they communicate. There are numerous possible styles. We offer the following three by Hart and Burks because the styles build upon the management "climates" mentioned in Chapter 7 and uncover the specific communication behaviors that constitute the three climates.

Hart and Burks compare and contrast three general types of communicators. *Noble Selves* are people who perceive that they should not adapt to other people or to situations in any way which violates their beliefs, values, or normal activities. Noble Selves stick to their personal ideals without variation and without adapting and adjusting to others.

---

*For Noble Selves, communication is a
"tool" to hammer home their ideas.*

---

At the other extreme, *Rhetorical Reflectors* are people who communicate as if they have no beliefs, values, or normal actions to call their own. They present a different image or reflection of themselves to every person and situation. Rhetorical Reflectors mold themselves to others' wishes, with no personal scruples to follow.

---

*For Rhetorical Reflectors, communication is a
"mirror" to satisfy the vanity of other people.*

---

In contrast to both extremes, *Rhetorical Sensitives* embody a concern for self, others, and different situations. Rhetorical Sensitives are people who accept personal complexity and understand that each individual is a composite of many selves. They attempt to balance self-interests with the interests of others.

---

*For Rhetorical Sensitives, communication is a "scale"*
*to balance the interests of various points of view.*

---

Rhetorical Sensitives moderate the extremes of Noble Selves and Rhetorical Reflectors because they are capable of:

- Taking on a large number of organizational roles.

- Avoiding rigid patterns of communication.

- Respecting the needs of other people, but not sacrificing their own ideas and feelings to placate others.

- Appreciating that ideas and feelings should be expressed only when it is appropriate to do so.

- Searching for the best way to communicate ideas and feelings.

---

*Unlike the communication styles of Noble Selves and Rhetorical*
*Reflectors, Rhetorical Sensitives improve their ability*
*as managers or leaders to motivate, to listen to the*
*relational content of communication, and to process*
*effectively the information they receive.*

---

First, Rhetorical Sensitives appreciate that every organizational message—oral and written—is *polysemous*. That is, it has different levels of meaning. As this book has emphasized, communication messages have "meaning" at the cognitive or "command" level; in other words, they have content. But messages also have meanings at emotional and "relational" levels.

In formal organizations, calm rationality is often valued and emotion denigrated. It is assumed that emotional displays are suppressed. But managers can accurately send and understand messages only if they are able to manage underlying emotions. Messages always say something about the sender's working relationship with the receiver, with other members of the organization, and with the organization itself.

---

*Rhetorical Sensitive managers understand that messages reveal what*
*people believe they can contribute to the organization, who are their*
*allies, who has power over them, and who is worthy of respect.*

---

Second, Rhetorical Sensitive managers appreciate the importance of norms and are thus open to more accurate and more complete information about the possible effects which underlie communication messages. These "hidden rules" of an organization are revealed by the timing of messages, the audiences that are selected or avoided, and the arguments that are proposed or suppressed. Without this understanding, managers cannot produce the kinds of motivational effects they want or effectively interpret the information of others.

For example, when an old-timer tells a new manager that "That's a pretty good idea, for a rookie," it can mean a variety of things. It could be focused on the information (it is a good idea). It could be focused on emotion (the old-timer's pride in his or her mentoree). Or it could be focused on relationship (to establish that the new manager is a subordinate).

Third, Rhetorical Sensitives learn to listen for *organizational implications* that messages contain. Two major kinds of implications are present in almost all messages. The first involves the *function* of the message. Some messages are decision-making messages. They call for responses that focus on the problem. Responses that express disagreement are appropriate if objective and solution-oriented.

But other messages only seem like decision-making messages. They can actually be ritualistic. For example, "What can we ever do to replace Alice?" does not really call for decision-making and the response, "Well, Fred could easily do quite well," would be inappropriate and might also reveal some damaging information.

The second kind of implication involves the *negotiation of organization roles.* Often, messages serve as invitations for others to affirm that they understand and accept their roles in the power structure of the organization. Managers who do not hear that implication may respond in ways that inadvertently challenge the hierarchy of the organization!

The risk to a manager's career development, to relationships with co-workers, and even to mental health is quite large and often depends on the ability to manage and to listen to multiple meanings in messages. If one wants to "communicate for effect," one must know how to respond, or the effect may not be the one desired.

---

*Successful career development for rhetorically sensitive managers means that they are more fully aware of the communication choices they need to make.*

---

In summary, rhetorical sensitivity and successful careers can be developed when managers accept a number of relatively simple attitudes about communication:

- Appreciate multiple levels of meaning.

- Understand that effective communication requires demanding practice.

- See how other employees have something worthwhile to say.

- Take into account how physical (phone calls) and psychological distractions (your own biases, words, or topics to which you respond emotionally, drawing conclusions before you understand what the other person has said) affect organizational communication.

## ◆ THE PURPOSE OF PART FIVE OF THIS BOOK

The purpose of the chapters in Part Five of this book is *to help you see how the key to successful career advancement is adopting appropriate attitudes and techniques.*

Chapter 17 will discuss how you can avoid some of the more common communication and human relations mistakes in organizations. Chapter 18 offers some choices for competent career development. Chapter 19 emphasizes the communication and human relations elements of a positive attitude. Chapter 20 concludes Part Five with a discussion about the necessary competencies for being a successful manager or leader.

# ◆CHAPTER 17
## AVOIDING COMMON COMMUNICATION AND HUMAN RELATIONS MISTAKES

Both new and experienced employees make communication and human relations mistakes that damage their personal progress. It is the purpose of this chapter to single out and fully explain the implications of six of the most common mistakes:

1. Failure to listen

2. Underestimating others

3. Failure to report or admit mistakes to management

4. Failure to provide your own motivation

5. Permitting others to turn you into a victim

6. Falling prey to negative drift

## ◆ FAILURE TO LISTEN

The art of listening is a basic communication skill. Many excellent books have been written on the subject. Your public library should contain several of these books. If you read just one, you will improve your competency in this area. Our discussion of the art of listening will be brief and to the point.

*The first step in learning how to listen is to learn how to concentrate.* Hearing is a selective process. Most people hear only what they want to hear. Your problem, then, is to listen to what is important and push other sounds to the outer edge of your hearing. There are so many sounds around you that you may not be picking up the ones that are vital to your happiness and success.

On the job, hearing is a matter of practical communication. When a supervisor or fellow worker wishes to transmit an idea, a warning, or a change in procedure to you, he (or she) usually does it verbally. There may be other sounds he cannot eliminate. It may be the end of the day and you may be tired. His words may mean one thing to him and another to you. Good, clear, accurate communication is never easy.

Let us assume, however, that the person initiating the message does the best job possible. Does this ensure that you will receive the message? Of course not! You are the receiver, and if your mind is focused elsewhere when the message is transmitted, *you may hear the sounds but fail to get the message.*

Advertising executives and specialists have recognized for years how difficult it is to get a verbal message home. This difficulty is most apparent in television commercials. There, the name of the product is often repeated six times in thirty seconds. If you are really listening, you might feel that such repetition is an insult to your ability to receive. You would be justified in having this reaction. But the advertising people do not assume that you are a good listener. They assume that you are a typical (that is, poor) listener. Consequently, to be sure the product name makes an impression, they pound it home through repetition.

Your supervisor is not an advertising expert, nor does she (or he) have the time to pound her message home. She feels she should be able to say it once and have it understood. She assumes you are a good listener.

Sometimes it is very difficult just to sit back and listen. There are three basic reasons why this is true. First, people are often so busy with their own thoughts and desires, related and unrelated, that they are 90 percent sender and only 10 percent receiver. When this happens, the communication system breaks down. Second, some individuals are self-centered. Instead of listening to what is being said, they are merely waiting for the speaker to finish so that they can talk. Getting their thoughts organized keeps them from being good listeners. Third, some people allow themselves to analyze the motives or personality traits of the person speaking and, again, fail to hear what is being said.

In business and industry, the ability to listen is often a matter of dollars and cents. A draftsman who doesn't hear an architect tell him to make a certain change in a blueprint can cause the loss of thousands of dollars when a bid is accepted on specifications that are not correct. A salesperson who fails to hear a message from a client, and as a result does not comply with an important delivery date, can lose not only the sale but also a valued customer.

Communication problems can also cost money in factories. For example, Daniel's failure to receive and retain the right message from his shop foreman cost his company a considerable amount of money. Here is the story.

On his way to his regular morning coffee break, and somewhat preoccupied with his own thoughts, Dan was stopped by his foreman and told to change the tolerance on a machine part he would be turning out for the rest of the day. After his coffee break, Dan returned to his machine, made an adjustment, and worked hard the rest of the day to complete all of the parts. The following day he was called on the carpet for producing parts that were too small. What had happened? Dan had been told to *increase* the size of the part, but he had *decreased* it instead. His failure to receive—and retain—the right message was a serious mistake, and it cost his company money in terms of both time and materials.

You can think of many other examples. It can even be said that when safety precautions are the subject of the message, the ability to listen can be a matter of life and death.

Let's look at your ability to listen from the viewpoint of your supervisor, who is, after all, the primary sender of important messages to you. Here are four questions you can ask yourself to determine whether you are a good listener:

1. Does your supervisor have to fight to get your attention?

2. Do you find yourself thinking about something else the moment your supervisor starts talking?

3. Does your supervisor insult you by repeating the message because he or she senses you are a poor listener? Or do you find you must go back and ask the supervisor to repeat it?

4. Do you sometimes feel confused about instructions given to you when you start to do the job requested?

If you can say no to these questions, you may be a good listener. If not, you should concentrate on improving. The following tips should help you.

1. Always look at the person who is sending the message; this will help you to concentrate and close out unimportant noises.

2. If your supervisor has trouble sending out clear signals, you must make the extra effort to listen more carefully. Although it is primarily his or her responsibility to be a good sender, it is still to your advantage to receive the message as clearly as possible.

3. To remember the message, jot it down in your notebook. Repeat it in your mind a few times. Put any change ordered in the message into practice as soon as possible. When appropriate, repeat the message to your supervisor.

4. Refrain from coming up with an excuse when you receive criticism. You will improve more if you listen to what you are doing wrong rather than quickly coming to your own defense.

5. Think, reply briefly if necessary, and then continue to listen, so that you receive the complete message.

6. Always ask questions right away if you don't understand something. If you don't do this, you may not fully get the message that follows.

7. If you find yourself in conversation with someone who is overly talkative, do not hesitate to interrupt after a polite period of time. If you do not do this, you may become so irritated you may not listen anyway.

Being a good listener is not easy. It will take a conscientious effort on your part. But one of the finest compliments you will ever receive from a superior will be something like this: "One thing I really like about Harry is that if you tell him something once, you know he's got it. You never have to tell him twice."

## ◆ UNDERESTIMATING OTHERS

The second of the six big mistakes, according to human resources people, is that of underestimating others.

A superior or co-worker may not appear to be doing much from your limited perspective. You might, therefore, wrongly assume that he or she is coasting. This could be a big mistake.

Here is a simple case to emphasize the point.

Henry accepted a job with a major metropolitan department store. After thirty days of training, he was temporarily assigned to work with Ms. Smith, the manager of inexpensive women's apparel.

Henry soon discovered that he was part of a rather hectic operation. Merchandise moved in and out of the department quickly. Ms. Smith was not an impressive person to Henry. Her desk was disorderly. She seemed to move in many directions at the same time. She seemed to spend more time than necessary talking to the employees.

Henry decided that he had drawn an unfortunate first assignment.

It was his good luck to meet a young buyer at lunch one day. From this woman he learned that Ms. Smith had the most profitable department in the store and an outstanding reputation with all top management people. Ms. Smith had trained more of the store's executives than any other person. It was then obvious that Henry had received one of the best assignments and had seriously underestimated Ms. Smith.

The new employee in this case learned a big lesson without getting hurt. He quickly changed his attitude toward his supervisor before the relationship was seriously damaged. He was fortunate.

When you fail to build a quality relationship with a supervisor or co-worker because you underestimate them, you may hurt yourself in the following ways. Your negative attitude may cause you to learn less from this person than you otherwise would. Co-workers may sense the mistake you are making and see your attitude as a sign of immaturity. The individual you have misjudged may sense your attitude and resent it, causing a serious human relations problem.

If you are a new employee or have recently accepted a new assignment, remind yourself that you are in the poorest position to estimate the power, influence, and contribution that others are making to the organization, *especially when these people are already in management positions.* You will be smart to avoid prejudging others. Different people make different contributions to the growth and profit of an organization. Top management can see this, but you usually cannot.

If the temptation is too great and you must at times question the effectiveness of others, keep your impressions to yourself. You can easily trap yourself by being a Monday morning quarterback. Underestimating the value of others can keep you from building relationships that are important to your personal progress.

## ◆ FAILURE TO REPORT OR ADMIT MISTAKES TO MANAGEMENT

A third common human relations mistake is failure to admit or report to management personal errors in judgment or violations of company procedures, rules, and regulations.

Everyone makes minor blunders from time to time. Even a good employee is not perfect. Precise and methodical people sometimes make mistakes in calculations. Logical thinkers who pride themselves on their scientific approach to decision-making sometimes make an error in judgment. A conscientious person who is very loyal to the organization will, on occasion, violate a company rule or regulation before he or she knows it.

These things happen to the best of people, and unless you are a most unusual person, they will happen to you. These little mistakes will not damage your career if you admit them openly. They can, however, cause considerable damage if you try to cover them up and in so doing compound the original mistake. To illustrate, let us take the incident of the dented fender.

Ken worked for a large banking organization. One of his numerous responsibilities was to deliver documents to various branch operations in the banking system. To do this, he checked out a company car from the transportation department.

On one such assignment, Ken dented the fender of a company car while backing out of a crowded parking lot. He knew that he should report the damage to the dispatcher, but the dent was so insignificant that he thought it would go unnoticed. Why make a federal case out of a little scratch? Why spoil a clean record with the company over something so unimportant?

Two days later Ken was called into the private office of his department manager. It was an embarrassing twenty minutes. He had to admit that he was responsible for the damage and that he had broken a company rule by not reporting it. The incident was then closed.

The slight damage to the company car was a human error anyone could make. The big mistake Ken made was in not reporting it. Looking back on the incident, he admitted that the damage to the car was far less than the damage to his relationship with others.

Most little mistakes, and sometimes many big mistakes, are accepted and forgotten when they are openly and quickly reported. Throwing up a smoke screen to cover them is asking for trouble. The second mistake may be more damaging than the first.

## ◆ FAILURE TO PROVIDE YOUR OWN MOTIVATION

The modern approach by management to provide the best possible working environment—*and then give employees the freedom to motivate themselves in their own way*—often leaves a few individuals on the sidelines unmotivated. It is a communication and human relations mistake to allow yourself to fall into this category.

New employees are expected to possess sufficient self-confidence to engage in the normal work process without always having to be nudged by others; experienced workers are expected to stay alert and productive without special counseling by their supervisors. Those who stand or sit around while co-workers are busily involved in productivity set themselves apart and, in so doing, injure their relationships with both supervisors and fellow employees.

In the workplace, everyone is expected to be a part of the team and contribute at acceptable levels. Those who wait around expecting or refusing to be motivated leave themselves on the sidelines where learning opportunities and promotional possibilities are limited.

Of course, anyone can occasionally have an off day. But self-motivation is primarily an attitude of consistent willingness to do whatever it takes (within legal and ethical bounds) to get the job done while meeting established timeliness and quality standards. Initially, it may take some extra effort to get your internal (self-motivation) generator going. Be willing to try harder and go the extra mile for your organization without constant prodding. More than likely, your managers will be more willing to reciprocate.

## ◆ PERMITTING OTHERS TO TURN YOU INTO A VICTIM

When people are unfortunate and become victims of automobile accidents or needless crimes, they often pay a high price. The consequences can be similarly serious when we become human relations victims. Consider the following:

- Statistically only a small percentage of people become direct victims of serious crime. Everyone eventually becomes a victim of a damaged relationship.

- Financial loss due to robbery, fraud, or physical injury can be high. So can the loss of a career opportunity that results from unrepaired relationships.

- The emotional and psychological damage of being a human relations victim can sometimes be as traumatic as being a victim of crime. Becoming a victim of a damaged relationship can cause moodiness, loss of confidence, resentfulness, indignation, and mental distress.

There are three primary ways people needlessly victimize themselves:

1. When they refuse to correct communication and human relations mistakes quickly.

2. When they do not make an effort to correct a no-fault situation.

3. When they permit the emotionalism of a relationship conflict to churn them up inside.

Many times a conflict will emerge within a relationship and both parties will become increasingly involved in a process that accelerates to more damaging stages.

*Stage 1:* There is only surface damage, low "hurt" involvement. Restoration possibilities are excellent—no harm, no foul.

*Stage 2:* Emotional damage is usually more serious for one individual than the other. Restoration is more difficult.

*Stage 3:* As a result of lack of communication, conflict becomes needlessly severe. Both parties become victims. Professional counseling may be needed.

The process will vary depending on the individual and the nature of the conflict. Once started, however, it often becomes a continuous development, until both parties become losers. Thus, the sooner any damage—no matter how slight—is repaired, the better. Just as both individuals can become victims, both can also become winners.

To help the reader avoid self-victimization, the following suggestions are made.

- Read Chapter 11 a second time to learn how to release your aggressions harmlessly.

- Remember that the more meaningful a relationship is to you, the higher the risk of self-victimization should a conflict occur.

- A substitute phrase for *self-victimization* is *holding a grudge.*

- Let small irritations pass.

- Every time a relationship conflict occurs, ask yourself this question: *Who will become the ultimate victim?*

Obviously, as you become more competent at human relations, fewer conflicts will surface and there is less chance that you will become a victim. But once a conflict develops, you become vulnerable and the steps you take to restore the relationship are critical. If you are not willing to take action (regardless of who may be at fault), you may nullify much of the human relations progress you have made.

## ◆ FALLING PREY TO NEGATIVE DRIFT

Observation and interviews over the years have convinced me that there is a subtle but consistent pressure that pushes us from positive to negative thinking. This phenomenon, for lack of a better label, we call *negative drift*. Similar to a pall of black smoke that hides a sunny landscape, negative drift is a gloomy cloud that prevents us from seeing the more positive factors in our lives.

What are the causes of negative drift? Most people believe that negative drift occurs because there are more negative factors to contend with in modern society. For example,

- Jobs are faster paced and more stressful;

- There is more crime, violence, traffic, litigation, and bureaucracy;

- The media provides an overdose of negative images.

The premise, then, is that we all must live in an environment with more negative stimuli, and, if we are not cautious, we become more negative *without knowing that it is happening.*

What is the answer? Most people agree that a strong counterforce is necessary. The problem intensifies when we recognize that an opposing force must be sufficiently powerful to hold back negative drift. Negative drift can creep up on us without our knowing it and, at the same time, cause us to lose focus on the positive factors in our jobs and personal lives. In other words, it is more of a challenge to stay positive in our society today than it was in the past.

Reflect for a moment and select the most consistently positive person you know. Now ask yourself this question: Does this individual have to work at it each day to stay positive? Chances are that the answer is a resounding "yes." Even when people have few negatives in their lives they must continue to "prop up" their attitudes on a daily basis to keep negative drift from taking over.

# ◆ CHAPTER 18
## CHOICES FOR SUCCESSFUL CAREER PLANNING

There are two basic paths to a top management position. One is to join and stay with a large organization, climbing the ladder of success rung by rung. The other is to move from one company to another, improving your position with each move. Those who prefer to move up within the same organization are *stabilizers.* Those who prefer the zigzag route are *scramblers.*

If you go about it in the right way, you can usually build a rich and rewarding career as a stabilizer. The practice that makes this possibility attractive is called *promotion from within,* or *PFW.*

There is nothing new about PFW. It has always been the custom to move those who demonstrate that they are capable and responsible into higher positions when vacancies occur. If effective people are available, management usually wants to promote from within the company's own ranks. This policy encourages loyalty, provides security, and has other advantages. It should be remembered, however, that even companies that have such a policy may make exceptions on their own or can be forced into adjustments because of layoffs and reorganizations.

In order to understand the implications of the PFW idea in a given corporation, one must study the organizational structure. Each company has grown to maturity in a different way; each firm has developed a different "culture." Every company has its own interpretation and application of a PFW policy.

Because of this, generalizations are dangerous. The reader must interpret the following pages in the light of the policies and practices of his or her own company. It is important, however, to give the new worker a perspective on his or her career possibilities. The following triangle will get us started.

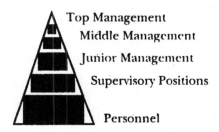

Top Management
Middle Management
Junior Management
Supervisory Positions
Personnel

This diagram could represent a business or an industrial or governmental organization. Size is not important. It could be a company with 200,000 employees or one with 200. Management—those people who are responsible for the leadership and direction of the company—is, of course, at the apex of the triangle. Some organizations divide management into four classifications: top management, middle management, junior management, and supervisory positions.

Top-management executives with giant concerns are usually the president and vice-presidents. Middle-management people are usually division heads and branch and plant managers. Junior management includes middle-management assistants, those whose positions fall just beneath the middle-management classification.* Next in line come the many supervisors.

Below the management level are many kinds of personnel, depending on the type of organization. In a manufacturing business we find different levels of technical people: engineers, technicians, skilled craftsmen, semiskilled workers, and helpers. In other kinds of organizations, there are different patterns and different backgrounds.

Supervisory positions, as illustrated here, can outnumber higher-management positions. There is usually a supervisory position for every twelve employees in an organization; in some companies the ratio is lower. The supervisory position is extremely important to the new worker, for in most cases this is the first position leading to upper management.

Now that we have seen the top of the triangle, let us look at the bottom. All organizations employ the majority of new workers at lower-level entry positions.

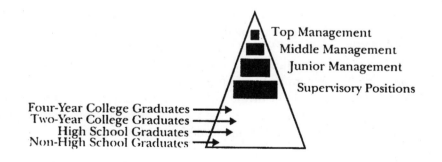

---

*To remain competitive and profitable, many organizations are currently eliminating middle- and junior-management positions. Front-line supervisors are having to assume more responsibilities.

Not all companies have four entry levels. Some have only two or three. The important thing is that all employees have an opportunity to grow. Each employee, regardless of where he or she starts, can and should move up in the organization. This is the meaning of PFW.

There are both advantages and disadvantages to building a lifetime career as a stabilizer in a single organization. Those who join companies with PFW intentions usually compete with those inside the company for better positions. They need not worry so much about outsiders who might be hired to fill positions they aspire to. Theoretically, everyone has a chance to compete, despite differences in education and experience. When someone at the top retires, a chain reaction can open up many positions all the way down the organizational ladder. This, of course, is possible only if reorganization does not take place or certain positions are not eliminated.

Organizations with PFW policies usually provide good training for their employees, so that they are ready to assume more responsibility when opportunities arise. This usually means that more on-the-job time is spent on training of all kinds. It also usually means that such companies will encourage their employees to continue their formal education and will often pay the bills. Because of this, employees are less likely to be ignored or lost in the shuffle.

Just as there are many advantages, there are also disadvantages to working for a company that likes to promote from within. Many highly ambitious people claim that promotions come too slowly. People are trained too far ahead of time. There is too much waiting. These are usually the same people who claim that the best way to reach the top is to move from company to company instead of staying with one organization. They point out that it is also possible that while waiting for an opening, a reorganization can take place, thus eliminating the position you were preparing to occupy. Moreover, the human relations role is more critical because management and nonmanagement people seldom forget anything. In short, a person who makes a serious human relations mistake in a PFW company must live with it longer because the people affected will be around to remember.

In the rapidly changing present economic climate, organizations are beginning to realize that they must become more flexible if they are to remain profitable. In some cases, restructuring and massive layoffs have been necessary. As a result, the emphasis on PFW is much reduced; in some organizations, it has been discarded.

The scrambling, or zigzag, route to the top involves an entirely different approach to career planning, as you can see from the following illustration. Here are some of the advantages of the scrambling approach.

1. For those who are willing to move about geographically and who are sufficiently aggressive to make the effort to seek out profitable transfers, the route to the top can be faster.

2. Sometimes an individual can achieve a wider and more valuable learning background by moving from one company to another. In other words, he or she can learn something new in each company and take it to the next one. This is especially true in high-technology fields.

3. It is easier to leave serious human relations mistakes behind and get a fresh start. This might include unresolved human conflicts or personality differences.

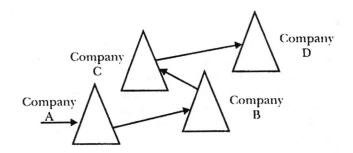

There are also disadvantages to the zigzag route.

1. Most people agree that it takes more energy to build an industry-wide reputation to ensure that profitable transfers come your way. There is also a degree of risk involved. You could discover, for example, that your most recent move was a mistake. Scramblers are not always successful.

2. Transferring often means uprooting the entire family and making profound personal and social, as well as professional, changes in your life.

3. Certain benefits, like profit sharing, cannot always be transferred from one company to another without loss or adjustment.

4. During periods of recession, when layoffs occur in many organizations, scrambling becomes more difficult and risky. Extra research and more caution is a good idea.

As you plan your career, take the following human relations factors into consideration.

• The longer you stay with a growing company, the more opportunities you will have, provided that you continue to learn and to maintain good horizontal and vertical relationships.

- Moving horizontally into every possible department is a good idea, whether the move gives you an immediate pay increase or not. Not only will you improve your knowledge base, you will also be in a position to build new relationships that can help your career progress.

- Discover and study the various channels of promotion in your company. Attempt to move up through the channel that best suits your ability. Set the stage for this through your human relations skills.

- Within bounds, do not fear being aggressive. Submit ideas that have been well researched. Communicate upward. Demonstrate your human relations skills at every opportunity.

- When a position becomes vacant, let management know in the right way that you are interested. Do not assume that they know. It doesn't hurt your relationships with others to ask.

- Cultivate and maintain relationships outside your organization, especially with people in professional or trade organizations. If it becomes obvious that your organization cannot provide you with the growth opportunities you desire, these individuals can help you scramble.

- Keep in mind that the training you receive as an employee (whether as a stabilizer or a scrambler) may be preparing you to open a business of your own. Entrepreneurship continues to grow in the United States.

# ◆ DIFFERENT WORKING ENVIRONMENTS

It usually takes a few weeks before new employees are in a position to analyze their working environments and answer the following questions: Does this working environment (culture) fit my long-term needs? Is it within my personal comfort zone? Can I see myself moving up into more responsible positions?

In evaluating a working environment, the following issues need to be taken into consideration:

- Is there a profit-sharing or stock-option plan that causes employees to stay longer and be more protective of their respective roles and of the firm as a whole?

- How stable is the organization? Is the firm strong enough to withstand a takeover attempt by an outside firm? Is management sufficiently flexible to adjust to the economic winds of change?

- Is there a career class system within the organization? For example, hospitals have their medical doctors at one level, nurses at another, and nonprofessionals at another. Would you be comfortable in a similar environment?

- Would it bother you to work for an organization (e.g., a restaurant) in which the steady turnover of employees makes it difficult to build long-term relationships?

- What about off-hours work? Hospitals, restaurants, and many factories have shift work that has a major impact on lifestyle.

- Would working in a high-fashion environment be within your comfort zone? Some retail organizations and home office centers create a haute couture environment that some enjoy but others do not.

Although the more investigation that takes place in advance the better, many new employees discover that the working environment they anticipated is not suitable for them. As a result, they develop a new career plan that will eventually take them into their comfort zone.

## ◆ HAVING A PLAN B

A professional scrambler always has a Plan B that he or she can put into operation when needed. A Plan B is a well-thought-out strategy (including an up-to-the-minute résumé, outside contacts, and constantly updated skills) that will permit the scrambler to locate a better position with another firm in the shortest possible time.

In the past, stabilizers did not feel the need to have a Plan B. There are two reasons why this is no longer viable. First, stabilizers have discovered that scramblers have often substantially improved their career positions by having and using a Plan B. Second, organizational changes (mergers, buy-outs, restructuring, and so forth) have frequently left stabilizers holding the bag. Result? More and more stabilizers are going back to school to upgrade their skills and develop a formal Plan B.

This author recommends that both scramblers and stabilizers develop a Plan B for two reasons:

1. If the winds of change eliminate your position, you are prepared to move on to something better.

2. Just having a Plan B ready makes it easier for you to maintain a positive attitude where you are presently working.

Many workers either become discouraged with their progress or fearful that their jobs will be eliminated without doing anything about it. When they develop a Plan B, they not only eliminate some of the fear that goes along with losing a job, they also feel better about their current positions, their attitudes improve, they become more productive, and they receive promotions. As a result, there is no need to scramble.

# ♦ CHAPTER 19

## COMMUNICATING A RENEWED ATTITUDE

*Renewal* means to restore or refresh. Employees at all levels occasionally need to renew their positive view toward their careers, rejuvenate their approach to the type of work they perform, or reestablish their positive focus toward their organizations. Everyone, even the most optimistic individual, should, from time to time, go through some form of attitude renewal. To some, maintaining a positive focus is a full-time job.

Attitude renewal, at the first level, is often a daily process. For a few, moments of early-morning meditation are helpful. Others, who may get off to a bad start, call a friend in mid-morning for a "boost" and then start the day anew. Other forms of adjustment (regaining a positive focus) can take place at other points throughout a given day.

At a more serious level, attitude renewal can be a weekend project. You hear both employees and managers make statements such as: "I need a strong dose of weekend rest and recreation to get my attitude ready for Monday morning," and "Without the quiet time I enjoy during weekends, I would be a basket case Monday morning." Without periodic time off or weekend attitude adjustment periods, most people could not remain positive and productive in their work environments.

There are times, however, when even weekend renewals are not sufficient. A major overhaul may be necessary. This is true because now and then most individuals fall into an "attitudinal rut."

An attitudinal rut usually occurs when someone slips unknowingly into a pattern of negative behavior that, unfortunately, can continue over a long period of time. Although some days are better than others, the individual's focus is permanently skewed to the negative side of his or her perception. Obviously, remaining in an attitudinal rut can inflict severe damage on one's career.

Nevertheless, it is possible to fall into such a rut without knowing it. When you become physically ill, for example, your body sends you a signal—you get a headache, a fever, or pain—and you do something about it. When you slip into an attitudinal rut, your mind may be unable to send you a clear signal of distress because you are not in physical pain. Your co-workers or close friends may *want* to send you a signal, but it is such a sensitive area that they back away. As a consequence, some people stay in their attitudinal ruts for long periods.

> Over two years ago, when he was passed over for a promotion he thought he deserved, George pushed himself into a negative rut. He is in the same trough today. Even if there were some easy way to tell George that he is negative, he would deny it because he has been in this special rut so long that he thinks his behavior is normal. As a result, he cannot see that he is his own worst enemy.

## ◆ ATTITUDE AND STRESS

Job stress is self-imposed when workers set too many difficult goals for themselves and, as a result, move in an unorganized manner in too many directions at the same time. Most stress, however, is caused by the job itself. Some jobs—such as those of television news personnel, air traffic controllers, and police officers—are recognized as stressful. Excessive stress can cause job burnout, which results in impairment of work productivity. Warning signals include feelings of frustration (Chapter 11), emotional outbursts, and withdrawal. Human relationships usually deteriorate.

*Do those who maintain positive attitudes handle stress better than others?* Generally speaking, yes. When you focus on the positive elements of a work environment, you are more apt to envision yourself as a winner. Result? You laugh more and find it easier to relax. With these behavioral patterns, less stress affects the individual, and the stress that does occur is dissipated with less damage. In contrast, those with behavioral patterns connected with negative attitudes appear to open the door to additional stress and hold the pressure created within themselves longer.

Although the more stress that can be removed from any job (fewer deadlines, unreasonable demands, human conflicts) the better, all jobs generate some stress. Whatever the stress level may be, those who concentrate on maintaining good co-worker relationships seem to handle it with less harm to themselves.

*Can returning to a positive from a negative attitude be considered an antidote to excessive stress and possible burnout?* To a limited extent, yes. When excessive stress eventually gets to workers, they often focus excessively on the negative factors always present. After an attitude-renewal program takes place (vacation, counseling, self-help), these same people see the more positive factors present; in this sense, returning to their positive attitude constitutes an antidote.

The Attitude Adjustment Scale that follows is designed to help you assess the current condition of your own attitude. View it in the same manner you would one of those electronic instruments used to determine if your car engine needs a tune-up. The results might send you a signal that, with a few adjustments, you could be a more positive, successful, and happy person.

## ATTITUDE ADJUSTMENT SCALE

Please use this exercise to rate your current attitude. Read the statement and circle the number where you feel you belong. If you circle a 10, you are saying your attitude could not be better in this area; if you circle a 1, you are saying it could not be worse.

| | *High* (Positive) | *Low* (Negative) |
|---|---|---|
| 1. I'm not going to ask, but my honest guess is that my boss would now rate my general attitude as . . . | 10 9 8 7 6 5 4 | 3 2 1 |
| 2. Given a chance, co-workers and family would rate my attitude as a . . . | 10 9 8 7 6 5 4 | 3 2 1 |
| 3. I would rate my attitude as a . . . | 10 9 8 7 6 5 4 | 3 2 1 |
| 4. In dealing with others, I believe my current effectiveness rates a . . . | 10 9 8 7 6 5 4 | 3 2 1 |
| 5. My current creativity level rates . . . | 10 9 8 7 6 5 4 | 3 2 1 |
| 6. If there were a meter to gauge my sense of humor at this stage, I believe it would read close to a . . . | 10 9 8 7 6 5 4 | 3 2 1 |
| 7. My recent disposition—the patience and sensitivity I show to others—deserves a rating of . . . | 10 9 8 7 6 5 4 | 3 2 1 |
| 8. For not letting little things bother me recently, I deserve a . . . | 10 9 8 7 6 5 4 | 3 2 1 |
| 9. Based on the number of compliments I've received lately, I deserve a . . . | 10 9 8 7 6 5 4 | 3 2 1 |
| 10. I would rate my enthusiasm toward my job and life in general during the past few weeks as a . . . | 10 9 8 7 6 5 4 | 3 2 1 |

TOTAL SCORE

A score of 90 or over is a signal that your attitude is "in tune," and no adjustments are necessary; a score between 70 and 90 is a signal that minor adjustments may help; a score under 50 indicates that a complete overhaul may be required.

Regardless of how you rated yourself on the scale, the attitude-adjustment techniques that follow can help you become a more positive and effective individual.

## Adjustment 1: Employ the Flip-Side Technique

The pivotal factor between being positive or negative is often a sense of humor. Attitude and humor have a symbiotic relationship. The more you develop your sense of humor, the more positive you will become. The more positive you become, the better your sense of humor will be. It's a happy arrangement.

Some people successfully use the "flip-side technique" to maintain and enhance their sense of humor. When a "negative" enters their lives, they immediately flip the problem over (as you would a phonograph record) and look for whatever humor may exist on the other side. When they succeed, these clever individuals are able to minimize the negative impact the problem has on their positive attitude.

> Jim, a software spreadsheet specialist, was devastated when he walked into his apartment. Everything was in shambles, and he quickly discovered that some valuable possessions were missing. After assessing the situation, Jim called Mary and said, "I think I have figured out a way for us to take that vacation trip to Mexico. I've just been robbed, but my homeowner's insurance is paid up. Why not come over and help me clean up while we finalize our plans?"

Humor in any form resists negative forces. It can restore your positive attitude and help you maintain a more balanced perspective on life.

How do you define a sense of humor?

A sense of humor is an attitudinal quality (mental focus) that encourages an individual to discover humor others may not see in the same situation. It is a philosophy that says: "If you take life too seriously, it will pull you down. Force yourself to pull back and laugh at the human predicament."

Countless incidents, which you could improve with a humorous twist, occur in your life each day. They will pass you by, however, unless you educate your attitude to see them. To help you do this, it might be helpful to give this mental set a special name. My nomination is *funny focus*. It may sound frivolous, but it describes what some wise people are actually able to do.

> "Susan always adjusts more quickly because she directs that strange mind of hers to the funny side."

> "Sam is good company because he has the unique capacity to find humor in any situation."

Those who receive such compliments nurture a funny focus that permits them to create a more positive perspective. This focus is their antidote to negative situations.

How can you improve your attitude through a greater sense of humor? How can you develop a funny focus that will fall within your comfort zone? Recognizing the following should help.

*Humor is an inside job.* Humor is not something that is natural for one person and unnatural for another. One individual is not blessed with a reservoir of humor waiting to be released, while another is left to cry. A sense of humor is created. With practice, anyone can do it.

*Laughter is therapeutic.* Just as negative emotions such as tension, anger, or stress can produce ulcers, headaches, and high blood pressure, positive emotions can relax nerves, improve digestion and circulation, and otherwise contribute to physical and emotional wellness. Dr. William F. Fry, Jr., a psychiatrist and associate clinical professor at Stanford University Medical School, maintains: "Laughter gets the endocrine system going." Of course, you can't laugh away all serious problems, but you can laugh your way into a more positive focus to help you cope with the problem. Laughter is soul music to attitude. It is a way of adjusting to a funny focus.

*A funny focus can get you out of the problem and into the solution.* Finding the humor in a situation usually won't solve a problem, but it can lead you in the right direction. Laughing can help transfer your focus from the problem to the solution. Using the flip-side technique starts the process.

## Adjustment 2: Play Your Winners

When retailers discover that a certain item is selling faster than others, they pour additional promotional money into this product. Their motto is: "Play the winners; don't go broke trying to promote the losers."

This same approach can help you adjust and maintain a positive attitude. You have special winners in your life. *The more you focus on them, the better.*

> Jason, at this point in his life, has more losers than winners. Having spent ten years in the work force, he is currently adjusting to a divorce, is deeply in debt, and has a car that is giving him fits. The only two positive factors are his job (Jason is making progress in the hotel management field he loves) and running. By pouring his energies into his career and running a minimum of six miles each day, Jason is able to maintain a positive attitude. He is playing his winners.

Each of us, at any stage in our lives, must deal with both positive factors (winners) and negative factors (losers). If you are not constantly alert, losers can take over and push your winners out of your mental focus. When this happens, you spend mind time dwelling on your losers. If this is allowed to continue, your attitude will become negative and your disposition will turn sour. *Your challenge is to find ways to push the losers to the perimeter of your thinking,* where you can live with them, perhaps permanently, in a graceful manner.

How can you do this? Here are three simple suggestions:

- *THINK more about your winners.* The more you concentrate on the winning elements in your life, the less time you will have to devote to the negatives. This means that your negative factors will receive less attention and, as a result, many may resolve themselves.

- *TALK only about your winners.* As long as you don't overdo it (or repeat yourself with the same party), the more you verbalize about the happy, exciting factors in your life, the more important they become to you. Those who talk incessantly about the negative aspects of their lives do their friends a disservice and perpetuate their own negative attitude.

- *REWARD yourself by enjoying your winners.* If you enjoy nature, play this winner by taking a nature walk. If music is a positive influence, listen to your favorite artist. If religion is a powerful force in your life, play your winner by praying.

You play your winners every time you think or talk or pray about them. But obviously, the best thing you can do is *enjoy* them. If you are a golfer, playing eighteen holes will do more for your attitude than thinking or talking about doing it.

**Adjustment 3: Give Your Positive Attitude to Others**

When you get fed up with the behavior of others, you may be tempted to tell them off and give them "a piece of your mind." This is understandably human. It is a better policy, however, to give others "a piece of your positive attitude." When you do this, you permit others to help you adjust your attitude.

> Sharon asked Casey to meet her for lunch because she needed a psychological lift. Casey didn't feel much like it, but she accepted and made a special effort to be upbeat. When the luncheon was over, Casey had not only given Sharon a boost, she felt better herself. Both parties came out ahead.

When you give part of your positive attitude to others, you create a symbiotic relationship. The recipient feels better, but so do you. In a somewhat upside-down twist, *you keep your positive attitude by giving it away.*

Everyone has opportunities to give his or her positive attitude to others. Taxi drivers who make their passengers laugh will increase their tips; employees who give co-workers deserved compliments increase their popularity; homeowners who send positive signals to neighbors eliminate problems with them when they see them; vacationers enhance their fun by making new friends simply by being pleasant to fellow travelers. Opportunities abound. The results are best, however, when the giving is toughest.

> It was a difficult Friday for Jane. Due to an emergency staff meeting in the morning, she was behind in her work. Just as she was starting to catch up, the computer went down. Then her boss asked her to finish an unexpected project before leaving for the weekend. When she finally left work, all Jane could think of was getting into her jacuzzi and forgetting it all. But she had promised herself to visit her friend Jackie, who was hospitalized. The temptation to drive straight home was strong, but she resisted and paid her visit. An hour later, Jane arrived home refreshed and positive. She didn't need the jacuzzi.

Each individual winds up a winner by giving his or her positive attitude away in a manner suited to his or her own personal style.

### Adjustment 4: Look Better to Yourself

You are constantly bombarded through media advertising to improve your image. Most messages state that only with a "new look" can you find acceptance and meet new friends.

> "Discover the new you. Join our health club and expand your circle of friends."
>
> "Let plastic surgery help you find a new partner."

Self-improvement of any kind should be applauded, but the overriding reason for a "new image" is not to look better for others, but for yourself. When you improve your appearance, you give your positive attitude a boost. It is not what happens outside that counts, but how your mind sees yourself.

The term *inferiority complex* is not in popular use today; however, we still relish the old textbook definition: *An inferiority complex is said to occur when you look better to others than you do to yourself.* In other words, when you have a negative self-image, you *make* yourself feel psychologically inferior when you probably are not.

The truth is that you often do look better to others than to yourself. There may be periods when you feel unfashionable, unattractive, and dowdy—but this does not mean you look that way to your friends. The problem is that you are communicating a negative attitude because you don't look good to yourself.

When you have a poor self-image, it is as though you are looking through a glass darkly. You feel you don't look good, so nothing else looks good to you. This occurs because your negative image psychologically distorts your attitude (the way you look at things mentally).

You see yourself first, your environment second. You can't remove yourself from the perceptual process.

Cedric gave up on ever having a good self-image when he was a teenager. All through college he was considered a reclusive grind. Approaching graduation, Cedric enrolled in a noncredit course designed to prepare students for a professional job search. Part of the program included doing a mock employment interview on videotape that would be critiqued by the instructor and fellow students. To prepare for this unwanted ordeal, Cedric purchased a new suit, had his hair restyled, and bought new, more fashionable glass frames. He practiced over and over at home. When his day arrived, Cedric did so well that he received compliments from all who viewed the tape. This recognition and support had a wonderful impact on Cedric. For the first time, he looked good to himself. Cedric's negative image was no longer a barrier to a good future.

The connection between a good self-image and a positive attitude cannot be ignored. In keeping a better image, it will help if you 1) admit that at times you may look better to others than you look to yourself; 2) play up your winning features—hair, smile, eyes, and so forth; and 3) make improvements in grooming—when improvement is possible.

## Adjustment 5: Accept the Physical Connection

Apparently no one has been able to prove conclusively that there is a direct relationship between physical well-being and attitude. Most, however, including the most cynical researchers in the area, concede that there is a connection.

More than any previous generation, today's young adults are aware of physical fitness. A surprising number incorporate daily workouts into their schedules. Their commitment to the "attitude connection" is expressed in these typical comments:

"My workout does as much for my attitude as it does for my body."

"Exercise tones up my body and tunes up my outlook."

"I never underestimate what working out does for me psychologically."

Many fitness enthusiasts depend upon exercise to keep them out of attitudinal ruts:

"I've renamed my health club The Attitude Adjustment Factory."

"I take a long walk to push negative thoughts out of my system."

"An unusually tough workout will often get me out of a mental rut."

No single group in our society deals more fully with the psychological aspects of attitude than professional athletes. Increasingly, athletes engage year round in sophisticated physical conditioning programs. They realize they must stay in shape to remain competitive.

"This same football team finished in the cellar last year. We made the playoffs this year because we have a new team attitude."

"I owe my success this season to my wife. She helped me adjust my attitude."

"My success this year is 90 percent due to a better attitude."

They must be trying to tell us something.

# ◆ CHAPTER 20
## NECESSARY COMPETENCIES FOR BEING A MANAGER OR A LEADER

Congratulations! By improving your communication and human relations skills and achieving greater insight into your positive attitude, you now possess the foundation upon which you can build a more promising career. Such a career may lead you into business management or a leadership role in a different career area of your choice. No one we know will argue with the following statements:

The more you practice sound human relations as an employee, the more likely it is that your superiors will promote you into management.

Everything you learn and practice about attitude and good human relations now will help you achieve a leadership position later.

Wherever you may be employed now or in the future, your superiors will probably be sensitive to the fact that you are building and maintaining better relationships with people than your co-workers and that you know how to operate effectively in a group. You have a double competency—you are skillful technically, you are also skillful with people. Observing this double competency, your superiors will naturally assume that if you are good at human relations at the employee level, you will also be good at the management level. It is a wise assumption. Let's look at what happened to Cleo.

A highly competent word-processor operator, Cleo concentrated on her personal productivity, but she did not neglect her human relations skills. She would frequently stop her own work to help someone with a problem. She would sometimes pitch in at the end of the day to help others get out an urgent report. Her efforts to help her co-workers did not go unrecognized.

Cleo was invited to attend a supervisory course on company time. Two weeks after the course was over, she became a supervisor. She was elated, not only because she had very little seniority, but also because she was the youngest person in her department. Her quick promotion made her respect her human relations skills more than ever.

The best thing about becoming more competent is that it makes one more self-confident. It happens every time. In short, the more you practice the communication skills discussed in this book, the more self-confidence you will build. Learning to establish strong working relationships with those who are older and more experienced than you is confidence building; being able to restore a damaged relationship is confidence building. The more you can prove to yourself that you are good at people skills, the less likely it is that you will be intimidated by others. Soon you will discover that you can deal effectively with sophisticated, experienced superiors at all levels; soon you will feel sufficiently confident to step out in front and be a leader. Jerry is a good case in point.

> Jerry, a sensitive and quiet young man, completed a self-study course in human relations because he wanted to develop more meaningful relationships with people both on and off the job. It was a personal thing with Jerry. He had no thoughts of ever becoming a leader. Such a role, he thought, was beyond his capacity. Yet within two years Jerry was so good at building relationships with co-workers that his personal confidence tripled. To both management and fellow workers he became a different person. When he was invited to become a supervisor, the only one surprised was Jerry himself.

When you demonstrate the self-confidence that practicing good human relations produces, new career doors automatically open. You may or may not choose to enter such doors, but it will be personally rewarding to know they are open.

Your transition into a supervisory role should be smooth, because all the human relations competencies you practice as an employee can be transferred to your new role. In fact, some skills will make more sense to you as a supervisor. For example, having tried, perhaps unsuccessfully, to build a relationship with a difficult supervisor, you will be more sensitive to the problem once you are there yourself. Knowing how a conflict between two co-workers can injure the productivity of all, you will pick up on such situations faster and intervene sooner. Knowing the rewards your supervisor could have given you but didn't, you will be more sensitive to your employees' needs for recognition. This is what happened to Geraldine.

> Geraldine was so disturbed by the behavior and insensitivity of her supervisor that she swore she would never become one herself. Then, because of a dramatic change in her personal life, she had second thoughts. Her rationale was as follows: Because the managers in my field are so ineffective, the opportunities should be limitless for someone like me, who is willing to learn how to be a good supervisor.
>
> So what did Geraldine do? She took a basic course in human relations skills and another course in management. As she did this, she made mental notes of the skills she would employ that her present manager did not. Her opportunity came sooner than she anticipated, and because of her basic

preparation, the transition was smooth. Geraldine has since received two additional promotions. What she learned as an employee provided her with a ticket to career success.

What about you? Should you, now that you are at least partly prepared, pursue a management role? If you are already in a beginning supervisory role, should you strike out for something in middle or upper management? The decision, of course, deserves careful consideration. Here are some thoughts you might wish to ponder.

*Accept the edge you already possess, but admit you have much to learn.* Many capable supervisors study human relations after they win their jobs. All those I talked to admitted that they started out with a handicap because they did not have a strong enough human relations background. This does not mean that human relations is the only thing a supervisor must know. There are many special supervisory skills that must be learned. Learning how to delegate, to conduct formal appraisals, to set priorities, to make decisions, and to manage one's time are critical supervisory skills.* If you wish to succeed in a management role, it will be necessary for you to become competent in these areas. You may wish to study these skills in anticipation of your first supervisory role.

*Management training is increasingly demanding.* Even if you prepare for and become an excellent supervisor, it is only a start. The more you may aspire to upper-management roles, the more training you should receive. The master of business administration (MBA) graduate degree has become the standard goal of many. Earning an MBA means taking demanding courses in statistics, computer science, management theory, finance, and other areas. If you decide to take this route to the top, keep in mind that in most cases you can earn an MBA while working full time.

*If you are intrigued with human relations, it is probably a sign that you will also like management.* Although there are many facets to a management job, most involve a great deal of interaction with people. A management job involves counseling, leadership development, and building a competent staff. Some corporate presidents devote more than 80 percent of their time to people problems. It is true that an executive manages resources and capital, but the first priority is people management. This will not change.

*The discipline factor may not be for you.* Those who are not in supervisory roles have the luxury of building rewarding relationships without having to assume the responsibility of correcting the behavior of others. Human relations at the worker level does not involve discipline. Some individuals who are outstanding at human relations are so sensitive to the needs of others and so compassionate in their dealings with others that they cannot correct or discipline

---

*The author of this book is also author of *Supervisor's Survival Kit,* 7th ed., 1996, Prentice Hall, Route 9W, Englewood Cliffs, NJ 07632.

those who get out of line. These people are uncomfortable in most leadership roles. They should, therefore, remain workers and make their contribution at that level. Not only will they be unhappy with the constant responsibility to discipline, they will probably not do it well.

*Could you make hard decisions?* Beginning supervisors must make many decisions each day. The further up the executive ladder they go, the more critical the decisions become. Most decisions are people decisions. And even those that are primarily productivity or financial decisions affect people.

The fact that you are good at human relations does not necessarily mean that you will be good at decision-making—in fact, the opposite may be true. For example, a manager may have to make a decision to give a layoff notice to a loyal and competent employee—perhaps even one with whom the manager has an outstanding relationship. There is some indication that the better one is at human relations, the more traumatic such a decision can be. You will want to weigh this factor carefully before deciding to become a supervisor.

*Management people are more vulnerable.* If you are a highly sensitive person (one reason why you may be good at building positive relationships with others), you may find it difficult to accept the criticism that goes along with a management role. Few, if any, managers are without detractors. In fact, whether or not a leader remains a leader often depends upon keeping detractors at a minimum or spotting them soon enough to bring them into the fold.

Do not misunderstand. Your human relations skills will help you to build good relationships with employees and thus minimize the possibility of negative reactions. You may never have someone under your supervision who becomes so disenchanted that he or she sets out to get you, but the possibility exists. Despite your own abilities, the role itself makes you more vulnerable. This statement is in no way intended to keep you from wanting to become a supervisor; it simply means that there are disadvantages you should consider in advance.

*Your personal attitude is more important—not less!* As a supervisor, maintaining your own positive attitude—staying out of attitudinal ruts—is critical. A negative attitude in front of employees is a luxury a person in management cannot afford.

Successful supervisors and leaders at all levels have the ability to create a positive force that pulls employees into a circle of involvement and activity. Once this force gets started, it seems to generate confidence among all team members and leads to constructive action and higher productivity.

How do you create a positive force?

Like a pebble dropped into a quiet pool, the power of your positive attitude gets things started. Thus, as a leader, your positive attitude is the *source* of your power. Your positive attitude communicates to those being led that they are headed in a direction that will eventually provide benefits. There are exciting goals within reach. Something better lies over the horizon. A positive attitude in a supervisor/leader builds positive expectations in the minds of workers, whereas a negative attitude destroys them.

The management/leadership challenge is, for many, exciting and rewarding. Those who have taken this career path claim that the challenge has forced them to recognize that their positive attitudes are, indeed, priceless possessions. Now that you have achieved new insights into human behavior and the importance of your own attitude, you are in a better position to decide whether management or leadership roles are for you.

Good luck!

# ◆ INDEX